TAKS MASTER®

Student Practice Book
Mathematics, Grade 5

for the Texas Assessment
of Knowledge and Skills

Lori Mammen
Editorial Director

D1451666

Editor: Sarah Nalini Mammen

Page Layout & Graphics: Pramilla Freitas, Rachel Friedrich, Jayme Salinas

ECS TestSMART™ Basic Skill-Building Lessons Software with Management System, Grades 1-10

Quality, Cost-Effective, Sequential Skill-Builders for Learners of All Ability Levels

	Number of Lessons	License for 1-5 CPUs	License for 6-15 CPUs	License for 16-24 CPUs	License for 25-up CPUs
Level 1-6 Reading	324	ECS2185-05	ECS2185-15	ECS2185-24	ECS2185
Level 1 Reading	54	ECS2045-05	ECS2045-15	ECS2045-24	ECS2045
Level 2 Reading	51	ECS2061-05	ECS2061-15	ECS2061-24	ECS2061
Level 3 Reading	54	ECS2088-05	ECS2088-15	ECS2088-24	ECS2088
Level 4 Reading	60	ECS210X-05	ECS210X-15	ECS210X-24	ECS210X
Level 5 Reading	58	ECS2126-05	ECS2126-15	ECS2126-24	ECS2126
Level 6 Reading	47	ECS2142-05	ECS2142-15	ECS2142-24	ECS2142
Level 7-10 Reading	81	ECS2169-05	ECS2169-15	ECS2169-24	ECS2169
Level 1-6 Math	172	ECS2193-05	ECS2193-15	ECS2193-24	ECS2193
Level 1 Math	17	ECS2053-05	ECS2053-15	ECS2053-24	ECS2053
Level 2 Math	33	ECS207X-05	ECS207X-15	ECS207X-24	ECS207X
Level 3 Math	24	ECS2096-05	ECS2096-15	ECS2096-24	ECS2096
Level 4 Math	35	ECS2118-05	ECS2118-15	ECS2118-24	ECS2118
Level 5 Math	24	ECS2134-05	ECS2134-15	ECS2134-24	ECS2134
Level 6 Math	39	ECS2150-05	ECS2150-15	ECS2150-24	ECS2150
Level 7-10 Math	68	ECS2177-05	ECS2177-15	ECS2177-24	ECS2177
Level 1-6 Reading & Math	496	ECS2207-05	ECS2207-15	ECS2207-24	ECS2207
Level 7-10 Reading & Math	149	ECS2215-05	ECS2215-15	ECS2215-24	ECS2215
All Levels Reading & Math	645	ECS2223-05	ECS2223-15	ECS2223-24	ECS2223

To order, or for a complete catalog, write:
ECS Learning Systems, Inc.
PO Box 791439
San Antonio, TX 78279-1439
Web site: **www.educyberstor.com**

Or contact your local school supply store.

ISBN #1-57022-376-9

Contents

Introduction

What's inside this book?

This *TAKS MASTER® Student Practice Book* provides appropriate practice review material for the Grade 5 Mathematics portion of the Texas Assessment of Knowledge and Skills (TAKS).

- The math problems reflect the kind of problems students might encounter on the actual TAKS

- The math problems cover a broad range of topics and ideas of interest to fifth-grade students

- The exercises test specific objectives and expectations for mastery of those objectives

- Each exercise is labeled for easy identification of the TEKS-based TAKS objective and expectation addressed in the problems (TEKS = Texas Essential Knowledge and Skills)

- Numerous problems and exercises in the book address the same expectation, providing repeated practice for students in varied contexts

- Selected problems include griddable response items as shown in the example below, which reflects the format used randomly throughout the actual TAKS

- For fifth grade, griddable response items include only 4 columns, a fixed decimal point is centered in the last column, answers range from 0 to 999, and students do not grid units

Record your answer and fill in the bubbles on your answer document. Be sure to use the correct place value.

This book also includes:

- A master list of objectives and expectations on the TAKS

- A fifth-grade mathematics chart of formulas and conversion factors

- A pretest to assess initial skill level

- An introductory page for each objective restating the expectations

- Complete answer keys

- Reproducible answer sheets—answer sheet A for use with most exercises and answer sheet B for use with exercises containing a griddable test item

How to Use This Book

Obviously, a strong curriculum and effective, varied instructional methods provide the foundation for all appropriate test preparation. Contrary to what some might believe, merely "teaching the test" performs a great disservice to students. Students must acquire knowledge, practice skills, and have specific educational experiences that can never be included on tests limited by time and in scope. For this reason, books like those in the *TAKS MASTER®* series should never become the heart of the curriculum or replace strong instructional practices.

Pretest to Assess Initial Skill Level

The *TAKS MASTER® Student Practice Book* for math includes a pretest with a selection of problems to test skills across the TEKS-based TAKS objectives and expectations. By conducting the pretest before beginning targeted practice, teachers can gauge the initial skill level of students along the objectives. Although the pretest only serves as a brief survey of skills, teachers can use it as a tool to focus instruction on students' specific needs.

Note: Students may record answers to the pretest on a separate Scantron scoring sheet provided by the teacher. The teacher can also elect to adapt the answer sheet provided in this book or instruct students to record answers on their own papers.

Targeted Practice

TAKS MASTER® books thoroughly address the final element of effective test preparation (targeted test practice) by familiarizing students with both the content and format of the test. With this kind of practice, students know what to expect on the actual test. This, in turn, improves their chances of success.

Other Suggestions for Instruction

TAKS MASTER® books can serve as springboards for other effective instructional activities that help with test preparation.

Group Work: Teacher and students can work through selected practice exercises together, noting the kinds of problems and range of problem-solving techniques. They should discuss common errors for each kind of question and strategies for avoiding these errors.

Formulating Answers: Teachers may encourage students to use scratch work to formulate their own answers on paper rather than simply using mental math or guessing based on the given answer choices. After solving a problem on their own, students can read the given answer choices and determine which one, if any, matches the answer they have recorded. If they cannot find their solution among the given answer choices, they can refer to their scratch work and determine their error.

Developing Test Problems: Teachers may create additional problems that cover skills in a different way than those provided in the exercises. Teachers and students also can select "test-type" problems from other assigned math exercises.

Developing Fundamental Understanding: Teachers can promote the recognition of mathematics in everyday life by developing problems relevant to students' daily experiences in the classroom and at home. Working through problems that relate directly to students' experiences fosters understanding of underlying processes and mathematical tools.

TAKS Mathematics
Grade 5 Objectives

Objective 1
Numbers, Operations, and Quantitative Reasoning

A. Use place value to read, write, compare, and order whole numbers through the billions place

B. Use place value to read, write, compare, and order decimals through the thousandths place

C. Generate equivalent fractions

D. Compare 2 fractional quantities in problem-solving situations using a variety of methods, including common denominators

E. Use models to relate decimals to fractions that name tenths, hundredths, and thousandths

F. Use addition and subtraction to solve problems involving whole numbers and decimals

G. Use multiplication to solve problems involving whole numbers (no more than 3 digits times 2 digits without technology)

H. Use division to solve problems involving whole numbers (no more than 2-digit divisors and 3-digit dividends without technology)

I. Identify prime factors of a whole number and common factors of a set of whole numbers

J. Model and record addition and subtraction of fractions with like denominators in problem-solving situations

K. Round whole numbers and decimals through tenths to approximate reasonable results in problem situations

L. Estimate to solve problems where exact answers are not required

Objective 2
Patterns, Relationships, and Algebraic Reasoning

A. Use pictures to make generalizations about determining all possible combinations

B. Use lists, tables, charts, and diagrams to find patterns and make generalizations, such as a procedure for determining equivalent fractions

C. Identify prime and composite numbers using models and patterns in factor pairs

D. Select from and use diagrams and number sentences to represent real-life situations

© ECS Learning Systems, Inc. ■ TAKS MASTER Math, Grade 5

Objective 3
Geometry and Spatial Reasoning

A. Identify critical attributes including parallel, perpendicular, and congruent parts of geometric shapes and solids

B. Use critical attributes to define geometric shapes and solids

C. Sketch the results of translations, rotations, and reflections

D. Describe the transformation that generates 1 figure from the other when given 2 congruent figures

E. Locate and name points on a coordinate grid using ordered pairs of whole numbers

Objective 4
Measurement

A. Measure volume using models of cubic units

B. Measure to solve problems involving length (including perimeter), weight, capacity, time, temperature, and area

C. Describe numerical relationships between units of measure within the same measurement system, such as an inch is $\frac{1}{12}$ of a foot

Objective 5
Probability and Statistics

A. Use fractions to describe the results of an experiment

B. Use experimental results to make predictions

C. Use tables of related number pairs to make line graphs

D. Describe characteristics of data presented in tables and graphs, including the shape and spread of the data and the middle number

E. Graph a given set of data using an appropriate graphical representation, such as a picture or a line

Objective 6
Underlying Processes and Mathematical Tools

A. Identify the mathematics in everyday situations

B. Use a problem-solving model that incorporates understanding the problem, making a plan, carrying out the plan, and evaluating the solution for reasonableness

C. Select or develop an appropriate problem-solving strategy, including drawing a picture, looking for a pattern, systematic guessing and checking, acting it out, making a table, working a simpler problem, or working backward to solve a problem

D. Relate informal language to mathematical language and symbols

E. Make generalizations from patterns or sets of examples and nonexamples

Grade 5
Mathematics Chart

Length

Metric	Customary
1 kilometer = 1000 meters	1 mile = 1760 yards
1 meter = 100 centimeters	1 mile = 5280 feet
1 centimeter = 10 millimeters	1 yard = 3 feet
	1 foot = 12 inches

Capacity and Volume

Metric	Customary
1 liter = 1000 milliliters	1 gallon = 4 quarts
	1 gallon = 128 ounces
	1 quart = 2 pints
	1 pint = 2 cups
	1 cup = 8 ounces

Mass and Weight

Metric	Customary
1 kilogram = 1000 grams	1 ton = 2000 pounds
1 gram = 1000 milligrams	1 pound = 16 ounces

Time

1 year = 365 days
1 year = 12 months
1 year = 52 weeks
1 week = 7 days
1 day = 24 hours
1 hour = 60 minutes
1 minute = 60 seconds

Perimeter	square	$P = 4s$
	rectangle	$P = 2l + 2w$ or $P = 2(l + w)$
Area	square	$A = s^2$
	rectangle	$A = lw$ or $A = bh$
	triangle	$A = \frac{1}{2}bh$ or $A = \frac{bh}{2}$

Inches

Centimeters

Grade 5 Pretest

1. How is the number 81,640,018 read?

   A Eight hundred million, six hundred forty thousand, eighteen

   B Eighty-one million, six hundred forty thousand, eighteen

   C Eighty-one thousand, eighteen

   D Eighty-one million, six hundred forty thousand, eighteen hundred

2. Which of the following is true?

   A 6.17 < 6.022

   B 2.012 > 2.024

   C 7.3 < 7.04

   D 6.11 > 6.018

3. Alicia was making a gift basket for her friend with 12 small gifts. She decided that $\frac{1}{2}$ of the gifts would be food items. What fraction is equal to $\frac{1}{2}$?

   A $\frac{2}{12}$

   B $\frac{4}{12}$

   C $\frac{6}{12}$

   D $\frac{8}{12}$

4. Toby had a box of $\frac{3}{4}$-inch nails, but the nails were too small for his birdhouse project. Which size nail is larger than $\frac{3}{4}$ inch?

   A $\frac{7}{8}$ in

   B $\frac{2}{3}$ in

   C $\frac{4}{9}$ in

   D $\frac{1}{3}$ in

5. What fraction of the model is shaded?

   A $1\frac{4}{10}$

   B $1\frac{4}{100}$

   C $\frac{14}{10}$

   D $\frac{14}{100}$

6. A biker rode 18.7 kilometers on Monday, 27.6 kilometers on Wednesday, and 14 kilometers on Friday. He took 15-minute breaks after every 10 kilometers. How many kilometers did the biker ride over the 3 days?

   A 49.3 km

   B 60.3 km

   C 75.3 km

   D Not Here

Grade 5 Pretest

7. Mr. Goldstein bought 6 boxes of candles. There were 8 candles in each box. Each box cost $18. How much did he spend on the candles?

A $48

B $108

C $144

D Not Here

8. A theater holds 864 people. The seats are arranged in rows, with 12 seats in each row. How many rows are there in the theater?

A 74

B 72

C 70

D Not Here

9. Which expression shows the prime factors of 81?

A 2 × 2 × 2 × 2 × 5

B 2 × 3 × 3 × 3

C 3 × 3 × 3

D 3 × 3 × 3 × 3

10. Shelly had a box of 12 glitter pens. She gave 4 pens to Zoe and 3 pens to Ally. She kept the remaining pens for herself. What fraction of the pens did she give away?

A $\frac{3}{12}$

B $\frac{4}{12}$

C $\frac{5}{12}$

D $\frac{7}{12}$

11. In math class, Roger had 6 homework assignments this month. His lowest score was 81, and his highest score was 95. Which is a **reasonable** total of all 6 homework assignment scores?

A 540 points

B 600 points

C 640 points

D 700 points

12. Ally bought 3 posters for her bedroom. The most expensive poster cost $15.99 and the least expensive poster cost $7.99. Which is the **best estimate** for the total amount Ally spent on posters?

A Less than $25

B Between $25 and $30

C Between $35 and $40

D More than $50

10 © ECS Learning Systems, Inc. ■ TAKS MASTER Math, Grade 5

Grade 5 Pretest

$(55 \times 3) + 40 =$

13. Mrs. Clarkson has 4 picture frames to arrange on her desk at work. If she places the picture frames in line, how many different arrangements can she make?

    A 12
    B 24
    C 120
    D 256

14. Look at the pattern of expressions listed in the chart below.

11 × 1	=	11
11 × 11	=	121
11 × 111	=	1,221
11 × 1,111	=	12,221
11 × 11,111	=	_____

    Which number goes in the blank space?

    A 22,221
    B 112,221
    C 122,221
    D 221,221

15. Which array of diamonds best represents a prime number?

    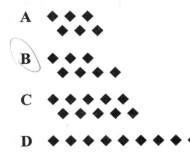

16. For the past 3 weeks, Selin has played basketball for 55 minutes every week. This week, he played basketball for only 40 minutes. Which number sentence could be used to find B, the total amount of time Selin played basketball in the 4 weeks.

    A $B = (55 \times 3) + 40$
    B $B = (55 + 40) \times 4$
    C $B = (55 \times 3) - 40$
    D $B = (40 \times 3) + 55$

17. The figure below is a rectangular prism.

    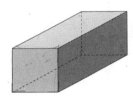

    Which statement is true?

    A All angles and faces of the rectangular prism are congruent.
    B The rectangular prism has 8 vertices.
    C The rectangular prism has 8 faces.
    D The rectangular prism has 8 edges.

18. Which solid figure could have a square base?

    A Triangular pyramid
    B Rectangular pyramid
    C Triangular prism
    D Cone

Grade 5 Pretest

Rotation
slide

19. In which diagram is the unshaded figure a rotation of the shaded figure?

A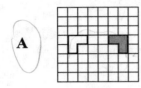

B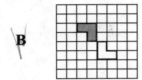

C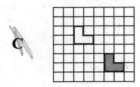

D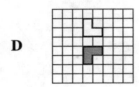

20. The figures on the graph show an example of a—

A rotation

B translation *slide*

C measurement

D reflection

reflection

21. Point J best represents which ordered pair?

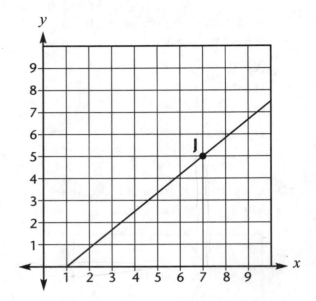

A (5, 7)

B (8, 6)

C (7, 5)

D (4, 7)

22. A rectangular prism made of 1-inch cubes is shown below.

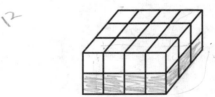

What is the volume of this rectangular prism?

A 8 in³

B 12 in³

C 24 in³

D 26 in³

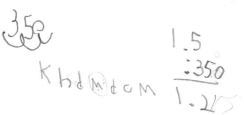

Grade 5 Pretest

23. Tim needs 350 grams of sugar for a recipe. A canister in his kitchen has 1.5 kilograms of sugar in it. How much sugar will be left in the can after Tim takes what he needs for the recipe?

- **A** 200 g
- **B** 500 g
- **C** 1.05 kg
- **D** 1.15 kg

24. Which unit of measure is $\frac{1}{8}$ of a gallon?

- **A** 1 cup
- **B** 1 quart
- **C** 1 ounce
- **D** 1 pint

25. The spinner is divided into 4 equal sections. What is the probability of the arrow landing on 2 when you spin?

- **A** $\frac{2}{3}$
- **B** $\frac{1}{2}$
- **C** $\frac{1}{3}$
- **D** $\frac{1}{4}$

26. A box contains 6 balls. They are the same size and same shape, but they have different patterns.

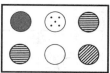

Which is a possible outcome if 4 balls are selected from the box at the same time?

27. On which coordinate plane does the number line pass through ordered pairs (1, 2) and (5, 6)?

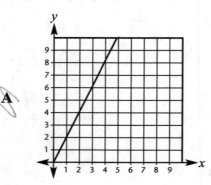

A

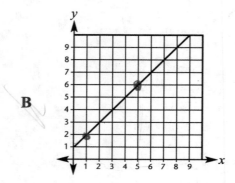

B

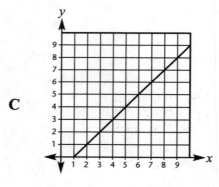

C

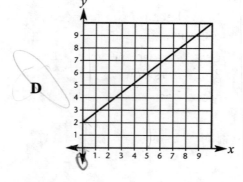

D

28. Anjali drew a diagram to show how many students in the class had bikes, video games, and CD players.

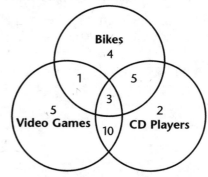

How many students have both bikes and CD players but no video games?

A 1
B 2
C 5
D 6

29. Anu, Myra, Jon, and Inez participated in a walk-a-thon to raise money for charity.

Anu	Myra	Jon	Inez
$240	$330	$270	$210

If each 🥾 stands for 30 dollars, which graph correctly shows the amount of money each child raised?

A

Anu	🥾🥾🥾🥾🥾🥾 180
Myra	🥾🥾🥾🥾🥾🥾🥾🥾🥾🥾🥾 330
Jon	🥾🥾🥾🥾🥾🥾🥾🥾🥾 270
Inez	🥾🥾🥾🥾🥾

B

Anu	🥾🥾🥾🥾🥾🥾🥾🥾 240
Myra	🥾🥾🥾🥾🥾🥾🥾🥾🥾🥾🥾 330
Jon	🥾🥾🥾🥾🥾🥾🥾🥾🥾 270
Inez	🥾🥾🥾🥾🥾🥾🥾 210

C

Anu	🥾🥾🥾🥾🥾🥾🥾🥾
Myra	🥾🥾🥾🥾🥾🥾🥾🥾🥾🥾
Jon	🥾🥾🥾🥾🥾🥾🥾🥾🥾
Inez	🥾🥾🥾🥾🥾🥾🥾

D

Anu	🥾🥾🥾🥾
Myra	🥾🥾🥾🥾🥾
Jon	🥾🥾🥾🥾
Inez	🥾🥾🥾

30. The sign shows the prices for the school store.

Pens	2 for 50¢
Pencils	3 for 25¢
Notebook	85¢
Eraser	32¢
Binder	$1.02

If a student spent a total of $2.27 before tax, which list most accurately shows the items purchased?

A 2 pens
2 notebooks
1 eraser

B 3 pencils
2 notebooks
1 eraser

C 2 notebooks
1 binder

D 3 pencils
1 binder

31. Madeline had $1.55 in her wallet. Her mom gave her $6.50 in spending money. In her piggy bank, she also had $5.65 in coins. Madeline added 2, 7, and 6. Compare Madeline's estimate to the total amount of money. Explain why her estimate is more or less than the actual total?

A More, because she rounded all 3 numbers down

B Less, because she rounded all 3 numbers down

C More, because she rounded all 3 numbers up

D Less, because she rounded all 3 numbers up

32. For his birthday party, Andrew has 48 candies to give his friends. He plans to put an equal number of candies in each of 6 bags. He also has 12 action figures to separate equally among the bags. What operations would he use to find the total number of items he will put in each bag?

A ×, ×, −

B ÷, ÷, −

C ×, ×, +

D ÷, ÷, +

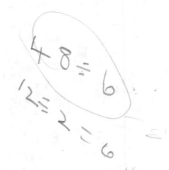

33. These are examples of lalas.

These are not examples of lalas.

Which figure below is a lalas?

A

B

C

D

Objective 1

Numbers, Operations, and Quantitative Reasoning

A. Use place value to read, write, compare, and order whole numbers through the billions place

B. Use place value to read, write, compare, and order decimals through the thousandths place

C. Generate equivalent fractions

D. Compare 2 fractional quantities in problem-solving situations using a variety of methods, including common denominators

E. Use models to relate decimals to fractions that name tenths, hundredths, and thousandths

F. Use addition and subtraction to solve problems involving whole numbers and decimals

G. Use multiplication to solve problems involving whole numbers (no more than 3 digits times 2 digits without technology)

H. Use division to solve problems involving whole numbers (no more than 2-digit divisors and 3-digit dividends without technology)

I. Identify prime factors of a whole number and common factors of a set of whole numbers

J. Model and record addition and subtraction of fractions with like denominators in problem-solving situations

K. Round whole numbers and decimals through tenths to approximate reasonable results in problem situations

L. Estimate to solve problems where exact answers are not required

1. Which number has a 3 in the ten thousands place?

   A 103,846

   B 91,342

   C 83,901

   D 34,176

2. How is the number 1,680,000 read?

   A Sixteen million, eighty thousand

   B One million, six hundred eighty thousand

   C One hundred sixty-eight million

   D One million, six hundred thousand eighty

3. Which of the following is true?

   A 10,842 > 18,402

   B 10,401 > 40,110

   C 11,946 > 9,461

   D 121,000 < 12,000

4. Which shows the numbers in order from **greatest** to **least**?

   A 81,460   81,640   84,016   84,106

   B 84,106   81,640   81,460   84,016

   C 84,106   84,016   81,640   81,460

   D 84,016   81,640   81,460   84,106

5. Which number has a 2 in the hundred thousands place?

   A 210,684

   B 120,846

   C 104,268

   D 102,468

6. What number is read as sixty-four thousand, eight hundred fifteen?

   A 640,815

   B 604,815

   C 64,815

   D 16,485

1. Which of the following is true?

   A $72,980 < 72,890$

   B $140,109 > 104,901$

   C $300,100 > 301,000$

   D $92,086 < 90,286$

2. Which shows the numbers in order from **least** to **greatest**?

   A 16,409 16,904 16,094 16,049

   B 16,904 16,409 16,094 16,049

   C 16,049 16,409 16,094 16,904

   D 16,049 16,094 16,409 16,904

3. Which number has a 1 in the millions place?

   A 4,013,467,902

   B 3,224,013,586

   C 2,021,309,674

   D 1,124,103,586

4. How is the number 131,401 read?

   A Thirteen thousand one, four hundred one

   B One hundred thirty thousand one

   C One thousand thirty-one, four hundred one

   D One hundred thirty-one thousand, four hundred one

5. Which of the following is true?

   A $32,094 < 30,294$

   B $26,436 < 26,346$

   C $14,610 > 14,160$

   D $12,810 > 21,180$

6. Which shows the numbers in order from **greatest** to **least**?

   A 46,412 46,241 46,214 46,421

   B 46,421 46,412 46,241 46,214

   C 46,241 46,421 46,214 46,412

   D 46,214 46,241 46,412 46,421

Objective 1
Exercise 3

Numbers, Operations, and Quantitative Reasoning
Expectation: Use place value to read, write, compare, and order whole numbers through the billions place

1. Which number has an 8 in the millions place and a 9 in the thousands place?

   A   181,429,216
   B   118,429,216
   C   811,492,126
   D   818,942,162

2. Which number is read as twenty-three million, two hundred eighty thousand?

   A   23,000,280
   B   23,002,800
   C   23,028,000
   D   23,280,000

3. Which of the following is true?

   A   1,001,100,001 > 1,001,100,100
   B   709,201 < 709,120
   C   604,010 < 640,100
   D   126,056 > 162,506

4. Which number is read one hundred eight million, two hundred fifty thousand, forty?

   A   180,254,000
   B   108,254,000
   C   108,250,040
   D   10,825,040

5. Which shows the numbers in order from **least** to **greatest**?

   A   121,106
       121,061
       112,016
       211,016

   B   112,016
       121,061
       121,106
       211,016

   C   112,016
       121,106
       211,016
       121,061

   D   112,016
       121,106
       121,061
       211,016

6. Which number has a 3 in the hundred thousands place and a 4 in the hundreds place?

   A   1,411,385
   B   1,311,485
   C   1,134,185
   D   1,113,485

Objective 1
Exercise 4

Numbers, Operations, and Quantitative Reasoning
Expectation: Use place value to read, write, compare, and order decimals through the thousandths place

-04   -30

1. The school nurse recorded the heights of 4 students.

Student	Height
R. Smith	60.73 in
T. Dawson	63.4 in
M. Singh	61.03 in
J. Montez	65.36 in

Which shows the heights in order from **tallest** to **shortest**?

A   60.73   63.4   61.03   65.36
B   60.73   61.03   63.4   65.36
C   61.03   65.36   63.4   60.73
D   65.36   63.4   61.03   60.73

2. Which of the following is true?

A   0.105 > 0.15   0.105   0.150
B   0.05 > 0.015   0.050   0.015
C   0.5 < 0.015   0.500 > 0.015
D   0.005 > 0.1   00

3. Which number is read as fourteen and fifteen hundredths?

A   14.51
B   14.15
C   14.015
D   1.415

4. Which of the following is greater than 0.04 but less than 0.3?

A   0.46
B   0.37
C   0.15
D   0.02

5. A hardware store sells shelves in 4 lengths: 0.5 meters, 0.8 meters, 1.2 meters, and 0.75 meters. The store displays the shelves in order from **shortest** to **longest**. Which of the following shows the lengths in the correct order?

A   0.5   0.8   1.2   0.75
B   1.2   0.5   0.8   0.75
C   0.5   0.75   0.8   1.2
D   0.8   1.2   0.75   0.5

6. Which number has a 6 in the tenths place?

A   121.006
B   121.36
C   121.63
D   162.31

1. For a science experiment, the teacher gave students 0.15 grams of baking powder, 0.09 grams of sugar, 0.2 grams of cornstarch, and 0.6 grams of flour. The teacher asked the students to use the items in order from **greatest** to **least** amount. In what order should the students have used the items?

   A   0.15   0.09   0.6   0.2

   B   0.15   0.6   0.2   0.09

   C   0.2   0.15   0.09   0.6

   D   0.6   0.2   0.15   0.09

2. Which of the following is true?

   A   0.018 < 0.2

   B   0.81 > 0.9

   C   0.118 > 0.31

   D   0.811 < 0.8

3. How is the number 121.23 read?

   A   One hundred twenty-one and twenty-three

   B   One hundred twenty-one and twenty-three tenths

   C   One hundred twenty-one and twenty-three hundredths

   D   One hundred twenty-one and two hundred thirty tenths

4. The chart shows the rainfall in San Antonio during 4 months.

Month	Rainfall
January	2.1 in
February	0.65 in
March	1.94 in
April	0.08 in

   Which shows the months in order from **greatest** to **least** amount of rainfall?

   A   January, March, February, April

   B   January, February, March, April

   C   March, February, January, April

   D   April, February, March, January

5. Which number has a 4 in the tenths place and a 1 in the thousandths place?

   A   0.014

   B   0.401

   C   0.14

   D   0.41

6. Which number is read as four hundred fourteen thousandths?

   A   0.104

   B   0.144

   C   0.414

   D   4.14

Numbers, Operations, and Quantitative Reasoning

Expectation: Use place value to read, write, compare, and order decimals through the thousandths place

1. Four students competed in the standing long jump. Joey jumped 1.08 meters, Judy jumped 1.4 meters, Ted jumped 1.25 meters, and Beth jumped 0.96 meters. Which shows the jumps in order from **longest** to **shortest**?

   A 1.25   1.08   0.96   1.4

   B 0.96   1.4   1.25   1.08

   C 1.4   1.25   1.08   0.96

   D 1.08   0.96   1.25   1.4

2. Which of the following is true?

   A 0.015 > 0.2

   B 0.401 > 0.5

   C 0.69 > 0.078

   D 0.08 < 0.075

3. Which number has an 8 in the hundredths place?

   A 800.016

   B 0.861

   C 0.681

   D 0.618

4. Which number is read as one thousand ten and sixteen hundredths?

   A 1,010.16

   B 1,000.16

   C 1,000.06

   D 1,000.016

5. Amy weighed different amounts of salt crystals in science class. She recorded the weights on a chart.

Sample	Weight
A	0.62 grams
B	0.25 grams
C	0.9 grams
D	0.3 grams

   Which shows the weights in order from **least** to **greatest**?

   A 0.25   0.3   0.62   0.9

   B 0.3   0.9   0.25   0.62

   C 0.9   0.62   0.3   0.25

   D 0.62   0.25   0.9   0.3

6. The chart shows the total distance hiked by members of a hiking club during 1 year.

Name	Distance Hiked
Seth	213.18 miles
Betty	213.8 miles
Charles	213.25 miles
Wendy	213.09 miles

   A prize was given to the hiker who hiked the greatest distance. Which hiker won the prize?

   A Seth

   B Betty

   C Charles

   D Wendy

1. Denise and James had identical candy bars. Denise ate $\frac{1}{2}$ of her candy bar. What fraction of his candy bar could James eat if he wanted to eat the same amount as Denise?

   A $\frac{2}{8}$

   B $\frac{4}{8}$

   C $\frac{3}{5}$

   D $\frac{4}{4}$

2. Which of the following is **NOT** equal to $\frac{1}{3}$?

   A $\frac{4}{12}$

   B $\frac{3}{9}$

   C $\frac{2}{6}$

   D $\frac{2}{4}$

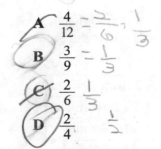

3. Mrs. Rogers cut a pie into 10 equal slices. Her son Jody ate $\frac{4}{10}$ of the pie. Which fraction is equal to $\frac{4}{10}$?

   A $\frac{2}{5}$

   B $\frac{2}{3}$

   C $\frac{1}{3}$

   D $\frac{1}{4}$

$$\frac{4}{10} = \frac{2}{5}$$

4. Mallory has 12 colored markers, but only $\frac{1}{6}$ of the markers work. Which fraction is equal to $\frac{1}{6}$?

   A $\frac{10}{12}$

   B $\frac{8}{12}$

   C $\frac{4}{12}$

   D $\frac{2}{12}$

5. Which of the following is **NOT** equal to $\frac{1}{2}$?

   A $\frac{5}{10}$

   B $\frac{3}{6}$

   C $\frac{2}{5}$

   D $\frac{2}{4}$

6. Cliff had 14 game tokens. He gave $\frac{1}{7}$ of the tokens to his brother. Which fraction is equal to $\frac{1}{7}$?

   A $\frac{12}{14}$

   B $\frac{10}{14}$

   C $\frac{7}{14}$

   D $\frac{2}{14}$

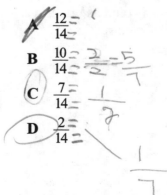

1. Which of the following is **NOT** true?

   A $\frac{1}{2} = \frac{3}{6}$

   B $\frac{1}{3} = \frac{4}{12}$

   C $\frac{1}{4} = \frac{2}{6}$

   D $\frac{2}{5} = \frac{4}{10}$

2. Which of the following is **NOT** equal to $\frac{2}{6}$?

   A $\frac{6}{18}$

   B $\frac{4}{12}$

   C $\frac{1}{3}$

   D $\frac{1}{2}$

3. In a parade, there were 12 floats. Only $\frac{1}{4}$ of the floats had animals on them. Which fraction is equal to $\frac{1}{4}$?

   A $\frac{2}{12}$

   B $\frac{3}{12}$

   C $\frac{4}{12}$

   D $\frac{6}{12}$

4. A box held 16 cookies. There were raisins in $\frac{1}{2}$ of the cookies. Which fraction is equal to $\frac{1}{2}$?

   A $\frac{12}{16}$

   B $\frac{10}{16}$

   C $\frac{8}{16}$

   D $\frac{4}{16}$

5. Which of the following is **NOT** equal to $\frac{4}{6}$?

   A $\frac{8}{12}$

   B $\frac{6}{10}$

   C $\frac{6}{9}$

   D $\frac{2}{3}$

6. A jar holds 9 gallons of liquid. Kelly fills $\frac{2}{3}$ of the jar with lemonade. Which fraction is equal to $\frac{2}{3}$?

   A $\frac{8}{9}$

   B $\frac{7}{9}$

   C $\frac{6}{9}$

   D $\frac{3}{9}$

1. Which of the following is true?

   A $\quad \dfrac{1}{2} = \dfrac{3}{5}$

   B $\quad \dfrac{1}{3} = \dfrac{6}{9}$

   C $\quad \dfrac{1}{4} = \dfrac{2}{8}$

   D $\quad \dfrac{1}{5} = \dfrac{4}{10}$

2. Which of the following is **NOT** equal to $\dfrac{3}{6}$?

   A $\quad \dfrac{6}{12}$

   B $\quad \dfrac{5}{10}$

   C $\quad \dfrac{5}{9}$

   D $\quad \dfrac{2}{4}$

3. Dori has 15 fish in her aquarium. Only $\dfrac{1}{5}$ of the fish are guppies. Which fraction is equal to $\dfrac{1}{5}$?

   A $\quad \dfrac{2}{15}$

   B $\quad \dfrac{3}{15}$

   C $\quad \dfrac{5}{15}$

   D $\quad \dfrac{6}{15}$

4. A cooler holds 9 cans of soft drinks. Only $\dfrac{1}{3}$ of the soft drinks are not colas. Which fraction is equal to $\dfrac{1}{3}$?

   A $\quad \dfrac{6}{9}$

   B $\quad \dfrac{4}{9}$

   C $\quad \dfrac{3}{9}$

   D $\quad \dfrac{2}{9}$

5. Which of the following is **NOT** equal to $\dfrac{6}{8}$?

   A $\quad \dfrac{3}{4}$

   B $\quad \dfrac{9}{12}$

   C $\quad \dfrac{12}{16}$

   D $\quad \dfrac{14}{16}$

6. There are 12 desks in a classroom. Only $\dfrac{1}{3}$ of the desks have chairs. Which fraction is equal to $\dfrac{1}{3}$?

   A $\quad \dfrac{8}{12}$

   B $\quad \dfrac{6}{12}$

   C $\quad \dfrac{4}{12}$

   D $\quad \dfrac{3}{12}$

Numbers, Operations, and Quantitative Reasoning

Expectation: Compare 2 fractional quantities in problem-solving situations using a variety of methods, including common denominators

1. At an ice-cream store, an adult's serving is $\frac{6}{8}$ cup of ice cream. A child's serving is smaller. Which amount of ice cream is smaller than $\frac{6}{8}$ cup?

   A $\frac{3}{4}$ c

   B $\frac{3}{5}$ c

   C $\frac{9}{10}$ c

   D $\frac{9}{12}$ c

2. Sarah made salad with $\frac{2}{3}$ cup lettuce, $\frac{3}{4}$ cup chopped carrots, $\frac{3}{8}$ cup radishes, and $\frac{1}{2}$ cup chopped tomatoes. She added the ingredients in order from **least** to **greatest** amount. Which ingredient did Sarah add last?

   A Radishes

   B Tomatoes

   C Carrots

   D Lettuce

3. A bookshelf has room to fit 1 more book no wider than $\frac{7}{8}$ inch. Which size book would **NOT** fit on the shelf?

   A $\frac{9}{10}$ in

   B $\frac{5}{6}$ in

   C $\frac{3}{4}$ in

   D $\frac{2}{3}$ in

4. David and Ann made blocks for their baby sister. The blocks were different lengths: $\frac{2}{5}$ foot, $\frac{1}{3}$ foot, $\frac{3}{4}$ foot, and $\frac{7}{8}$ foot. Which shows the lengths in order from **longest** to **shortest**?

   A $\frac{3}{4}$ $\quad$ $\frac{7}{8}$ $\quad$ $\frac{2}{5}$ $\quad$ $\frac{1}{3}$

   B $\frac{7}{8}$ $\quad$ $\frac{3}{4}$ $\quad$ $\frac{2}{5}$ $\quad$ $\frac{1}{3}$

   C $\frac{2}{5}$ $\quad$ $\frac{1}{3}$ $\quad$ $\frac{3}{4}$ $\quad$ $\frac{7}{8}$

   D $\frac{1}{3}$ $\quad$ $\frac{2}{5}$ $\quad$ $\frac{3}{4}$ $\quad$ $\frac{7}{8}$

Objective 1
Exercise 11

Numbers, Operations, and Quantitative Reasoning

Expectation: Compare 2 fractional quantities in problem-solving situations using a variety of methods, including common denominators

1. Four friends ate ice cream together. Carrie ate $\frac{3}{4}$ cup; Dale ate $\frac{3}{5}$ cup; Kyle ate $\frac{1}{2}$ cup; and Marsha ate $\frac{2}{3}$ cup. Which friend ate the least ice cream?

   A Carrie

   B Dale

   C Kyle

   D Marsha

2. The chart shows the dry ingredients needed for a cookie recipe.

Ingredient	Amount
Sugar	$\frac{2}{3}$ cup
Flour	$\frac{7}{8}$ cup
Chopped Nuts	$\frac{3}{4}$ cup
Raisins	$\frac{3}{5}$ cup

   The dry ingredients must be added from **least** to **greatest** amount. Which ingredient will be added first?

   A Sugar

   B Flour

   C Chopped nuts

   D Raisins

3. The chart shows the sizes of nails in a model kit.

Nail	Size
W	$\frac{3}{4}$ in
X	$\frac{2}{5}$ in
Y	$\frac{1}{3}$ in
Z	$\frac{2}{3}$ in

   Which is the smallest nail in the kit?

   A W

   B X

   C Y

   D Z

4. Landry bought more than $\frac{3}{4}$ pound of bananas. Which represents the weight she might have bought?

   A $\frac{7}{8}$ lb

   B $\frac{3}{5}$ lb

   C $\frac{2}{3}$ lb

   D $\frac{2}{4}$ lb

Numbers, Operations, and Quantitative Reasoning

Expectation: Compare 2 fractional quantities in problem-solving situations using a variety of methods, including common denominators

1. Frozen yogurt comes in 2 sizes. The smaller size holds $\frac{3}{8}$ cup of yogurt. How much yogurt might the larger size hold?

   A $\frac{1}{2}$ c

   B $\frac{1}{3}$ c

   C $\frac{1}{4}$ c

   D $\frac{1}{5}$ c

2. The chart shows the amount of oil used in 4 different cake recipes.

Cake	Oil
Almond	$\frac{3}{4}$ cup
Chocolate	$\frac{2}{3}$ cup
Vanilla	$\frac{2}{6}$ cup
Nut	$\frac{5}{6}$ cup

   Which cake called for no more than $\frac{1}{3}$ cup of oil?

   A Almond
   B Chocolate
   C Vanilla
   D Nut

3. During PE class, Susan ran $\frac{1}{5}$ mile; Jenny ran $\frac{2}{3}$ mile; Lauren ran $\frac{1}{4}$ mile; and Kim ran $\frac{3}{4}$ mile. Which girl ran the shortest distance?

   A Kim
   B Lauren
   C Jenny
   D Susan

4. Mr. Charles needs a piece of wood to replace a shelf in his bookcase. The wood must be longer than $\frac{3}{4}$ yard. Which length of wood is longer than $\frac{3}{4}$ yard?

   A $\frac{3}{8}$ yd

   B $\frac{4}{9}$ yd

   C $\frac{5}{6}$ yd

   D $\frac{7}{10}$ yd

1. Which part of the model is shaded?

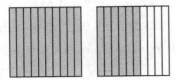

   A 1.6

   B 1.06

   C 1.006

   D 0.16

2. The model shows 0.5 shaded. Which fraction equals 0.5?

   A $\frac{5}{100}$

   B $\frac{15}{100}$

   C $\frac{5}{10}$

   D $\frac{50}{10}$

3. The model shows $\frac{1}{4}$ shaded. Which decimal equals $\frac{1}{4}$?

   A 0.75

   B 0.4

   C 0.25

   D 0.025

4. Look at the model. What fraction of the model is shaded?

   A $\frac{9}{100}$

   B $\frac{19}{100}$

   C $\frac{7}{10}$

   D $\frac{9}{10}$

1. What fraction of the model is shaded?

    A $1\frac{1}{4}$

    B $1\frac{1}{3}$

    C $1\frac{4}{10}$

    D $1\frac{1}{2}$

2. The model shows 0.15 shaded. Which fraction equals 0.15?

    A $\frac{1}{15}$

    B $\frac{15}{100}$

    C $\frac{5}{15}$

    D $\frac{35}{100}$

3. Which model shows $\frac{3}{10}$ shaded?

    A 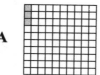

    B 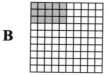

    C 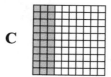

    D 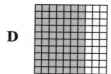

4. What part of the model is shaded?

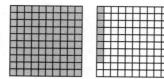

    A 1.82

    B 1.8

    C 1.18

    D 1.08

1. What part of the model is shaded?

   A   4.9

   B   4.09

   C   0.49

   D   0.049

2. The model shows $\frac{35}{100}$ shaded. Which
decimal equals $\frac{35}{100}$?

   A   0.135

   B   0.35

   C   3.5

   D   35.0

3. Which model shows 0.13 shaded?

A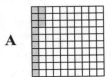

B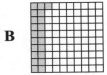

C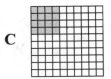

D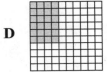

4. What fraction of the model is shaded?

   A $\frac{1}{5}$

   B $\frac{1}{4}$

   C $\frac{1}{3}$

   D $\frac{1}{2}$

1. What part of the model is shaded?

    A 1.24

    B 2.014

    C 2.14

    D 2.41

2. The model shows $\frac{5}{100}$ shaded. Which decimal equals $\frac{5}{100}$?

    A 5.0

    B 0.5

    C 0.15

    D 0.05

3. Which model shows 1.1 shaded?

    A

    B 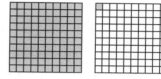

    C 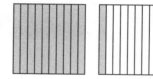

    D 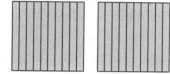

4. What fraction of the model is shaded?

    A $1\frac{7}{10}$

    B $1\frac{7}{100}$

    C $\frac{7}{10}$

    D $\frac{7}{100}$

$$\begin{array}{r} \overset{1}{\$3}.\overset{2}{5}9 \\ +\ 2.49 \\ \hline .89 \\ \hline \$6.97 \end{array}$$

1. Landen paid $3.59 for a new binder, $2.49 for a new pen, and $0.89 for notebook paper. How much did Landen pay for these school supplies?

   A $5.97

   B $6.77

   C $6.97

   D Not Here

2. On Monday, Bobby rode his bike 3.8 kilometers. He rode 4.6 kilometers on Tuesday and 5.25 kilometers on Wednesday. How many kilometers did Bobby ride during the 3 days?

   A 12.55 km

   B 13.45 km

   C 13.55 km

   D Not Here

3. While shopping, the Dotson family found 2 televisions that they liked. The first one cost $679. The second one cost $849. How much more would they pay for the second television than the first?

   A $270

   B $230

   C $170

   D Not Here

4. At Johnson Elementary School, there are 587 students. At DeWitt Elementary School, there are 715 students. How many fewer students go to Johnson Elementary School than to DeWitt Elementary School?

   A 272

   B 228

   C 128

   D Not Here

5. In January, Mrs. Potter's class collected 1,008 pounds of newspapers for recycling. In February, they collected 879 pounds. How many more pounds did they collect in January than in February?

   A 239 lb

   B 139 lb

   C 129 lb

   D Not Here

6. Last year, Josh was 54.6 inches tall. This year, he is 57.4 inches tall. How many inches has Josh grown in 1 year?

   A 3.2 in

   B 2.8 in

   C 2.2 in

   D Not Here

© ECS Learning Systems, Inc. ■ TAKS MASTER Math, Grade 5

1. The fifth-grade classes collected
aluminum cans for recycling. In
January, they collected 486 pounds.
They collected 308 pounds in February
and 396 pounds in March. How many
pounds of cans did the classes collect?

   A   1,170 lb
   B   1,190 lb
   C   1,195 lb
   D   Not Here

2. Martin has 715 baseball cards. His
sister Meg has 594 cards, and his
brother Peter has 458 cards. How many
cards would the children have if they
put all their cards together?

   A   1,777
   B   1,667
   C   1,657
   D   Not Here

3. Mr. Boyd's car has 8,137 miles on it.
Mrs. Boyd's car has 9,226 miles on it.
How many more miles does Mrs. Boyd's
car have than Mr. Boyd's car?

   A   1,199 mi
   B   1,189 mi
   C   1,089 mi
   D   Not Here

4. Blake carried 3 boxes a distance of
1.1 kilometers from the post office to
his house. The first box weighed
4.5 kilograms. The second weighed
5.45 kilograms. The third weighed
0.75 kilograms. What was the combined
weight of the 3 boxes?

   A   9.25 kg
   B   9.6 kg
   C   10.7 kg
   D   Not Here

5. Melissa bought in-line skates for $35.99
at the sports store. Her friend bought
the same kind of in-line skates at a
different store and paid $41.69. How
much more did Melissa's friend pay
than Melissa?

   A $5.70
   B $6.70
   C $14.30
   D   Not Here

6. Mr. Matthews has to travel 465 miles
on a business trip. He has already
traveled 286 miles. How many more
miles must he travel?

   A   289 mi
   B   221 mi
   C   179 mi
   D   Not Here

1. A recipe for punch calls for the following ingredients: 1.5 cups of orange juice, 2.5 cups of lemon-lime soda, 0.75 cup of cranberry juice, and 1.5 cups of pineapple juice. What is the total amount of juice and soda needed for the recipe?

    A   10.75 c

    B   7.25 c

    C   5.25 c

    D   Not Here

2. A shopper at a hardware store bought nails for $5.69, a hammer for $10.59, and lumber for $25.50. The shopper paid with a $100 bill. How much did the shopper spend on the items?

    A $41.78

    B $58.22

    C $141.78

    D   Not Here

3. Dana scored 3,174 points on a video game. Rajeen scored 2,865 points on the same game. How many more points did Rajeen need to equal Dana's score?

    Record your answer and fill in the bubbles on your answer document. Be sure to use the correct place value.

			.
⓪	⓪	⓪	
①	①	①	
②	②	②	
③	③	③	
④	④	④	
⑤	⑤	⑤	
⑥	⑥	⑥	
⑦	⑦	⑦	
⑧	⑧	⑧	
⑨	⑨	⑨	

4. At a grocery store, grapes cost $1.49 per pound. Apples cost $1.19 per pound, and bananas cost $0.69 per pound. How much would you pay for 1 pound each of grapes, apples, and bananas?

    A $3.37

    B $3.17

    C $2.17

    D   Not Here

5. Jessica received $50 for her birthday. If she buys a sweater that costs $15.49, how much of her birthday money will she still have?

    A $65.49

    B $35.51

    C $35.49

    D   Not Here

6. Danielle has 300 basketball cards, but Adam has only 141. How many more cards does Adam need in order to have as many as Danielle?

    A   259

    B   169

    C   159

    D   Not Here

1. Blaire earned 9,178 points on a video game. She played 2 more times and earned 8,964 points and 9,467 points. How many points did Blaire earn during the 3 games?

   A 27,609

   B 26,499

   C 18,645

   D Not Here

2. The chart shows points earned for a school read-a-thon. How many points did the students in third, fourth, and fifth grade earn?

Grade	Points
1	210
2	328
3	476
4	389
5	603

   A 1,458

   B 1,468

   C 1,548

   D Not Here

3. Mr. Sandoval bought a magazine that cost $2.95. If he gave the clerk a $20 bill, how much change did he receive?

   A $18.05

   B $17.95

   C $17.05

   D Not Here

4. Ronnie competed in the running long jump on field day. His first jump was 11.25 feet. His second jump was 13.8 feet. His third jump was 13.95 feet. What was the total distance for his jumps?

   A 39 ft

   B 38 ft

   C 28.6 ft

   D Not Here

5. A band gave 3 concerts. At the first concert, there were 815 people in the audience. At the second concert, there were 1,902. At the third, there were 968. What was the total number of people who attended the 3 concerts?

   A 3,665

   B 3,785

   C 3,885

   D Not Here

6. Mrs. Joseph wants to fence her property. She will need 400 meters of fencing. The store only has 235.8 meters of the fencing she wants to buy. How much more fencing does the store need to order for Mrs. Joseph?

   A 164.2 m

   B 174.2 m

   C 274.2 m

   D Not Here

Objective 1
Exercise 21

Numbers, Operations, and Quantitative Reasoning

Expectation: Use multiplication to solve problems involving whole numbers (no more than 3 digits times 2 digits without technology)

1. A grocery store received a shipment of 52 cases of granola bars. There were 36 boxes of granola bars in each case and 8 granola bars in each box. How many boxes of granola bars did the store receive?

   A 288

   B 1,672

   C 1,872

   D Not Here

2. Mr. Jenson bought 15 boxes of pencils. There were 24 pencils in each box. Each box cost $3. How much did he spend on the pencils?

   A $35

   B $45

   C $1,080

   D Not Here

3. A store owner bought a new book rack. She can display 18 books on each row. The rack has 12 rows. Each book costs $5. How many books can the store owner display on the rack?

   Record your answer and fill in the bubbles on your answer document. Be sure to use the correct place value.

			.
⓪	⓪	⓪	
①	①	①	
②	②	②	
③	③	③	
④	④	④	
⑤	⑤	⑤	
⑥	⑥	⑥	
⑦	⑦	⑦	
⑧	⑧	⑧	
⑨	⑨	⑨	

4. Ms. Peterson teaches art to 103 students. Each student will use 63 tiles to make a mosaic. How many tiles will Ms. Peterson need for all the students?

   A 6,804

   B 6,704

   C 171

   D Not Here

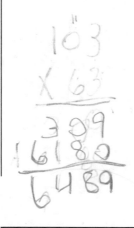

Objective 1
Exercise 22

Numbers, Operations, and Quantitative Reasoning

Expectation: Use multiplication to solve problems involving whole numbers (no more than 3 digits times 2 digits without technology)

1. A school orders copy paper by the case. Each case costs $35 and has 12 packages of paper. If the school orders 36 cases, how many packages of paper will it receive?

    A   218

    B   422

    C   432

    D   Not Here

2. A large football stadium has 43 rows of seats on 1 side. There are 213 seats in each row. How many people can be seated on that side of the stadium?

    A   9,169

    B   9,159

    C   9,059

    D   Not Here

3. A restaurant prepared 86 trays of sandwiches for a large party of 200 guests. Each tray had 34 small sandwiches. How many sandwiches did the restaurant make?

    A   2,804

    B   2,924

    C   2,964

    D   Not Here

4. Several fifth-grade students went on a field trip to the city museum. Each bus held 45 students. The students filled 8 buses. How many fifth-grade students went on the field trip?

    A   320

    B   360

    C   400

    D   Not Here

$$\begin{array}{r} 86 \\ \times\ 34 \\ \hline 344 \\ 3580 \\ \hline 2{,}924 \end{array}$$

Numbers, Operations, and Quantitative Reasoning

Expectation: Use multiplication to solve problems involving whole numbers (no more than 3 digits times 2 digits without technology)

1. The roller coaster at an amusement park holds 46 riders. During 1 month, the roller coaster ran 709 times. If all the seats were filled each time, how many people rode the roller coaster during that month?

   A   32,614

   B   32,514

   C   32,264

   D   Not Here

2. Mrs. Murphy's class took a field trip to Sea World. Only 23 students went on the trip. If each student paid $15 for a ticket, what was the total cost for all of the students?

   A $335

   B $345

   C $355

   D   Not Here

3. Jordan baked 7 batches of cookies for a bake sale. There were 36 cookies in 1 batch. How many cookies did Jordan bake?

   A   43

   B   242

   C   262

   D   Not Here

4. Mrs. Goldman, the principal, wants to make a holiday ornament for each teacher in the school. She will use 73 small glass beads on each ornament. There are 900 students and 48 teachers in the school. How many glass beads will Mrs. Goldman need?

   A   3,384

   B   3,404

   C   3,504

   D   Not Here

Numbers, Operations, and Quantitative Reasoning

Expectation: Use multiplication to solve problems involving whole numbers (no more than 3 digits times 2 digits without technology)

1. At Jefferson Elementary School, there are 37 classes. Each class has 26 students. There are 40 teachers at the school. What is the total number of students at Jefferson Elementary School?

   A   63

   B   822

   C   962

   D   Not Here

2. Cherisse made 112 food baskets for her grocery store. She put 30 items of food in each basket. What is the total number of food items Cherisse used to make the baskets?

   A   3,360

   B   3,362

   C   3,460

   D   Not Here

3. Katia collects postage stamps. She ordered 7 sets of stamps to add to her collection. Each set had 15 stamps and cost $4.00. How many stamps did Katia get in her order?

   Record your answer and fill in the bubbles on your answer document. Be sure to use the correct place value.

4. Jay's favorite basketball player averaged 28 points in each of his last 20 games. How many points did the basketball player make in all 20 games?

   A   56

   B   460

   C   560

   D   Not Here

Numbers, Operations, and Quantitative Reasoning

Expectation: Use division to solve problems involving whole numbers (no more than 2-digit divisors and 3-digit dividends without technology)

1. A theater has 968 seats. The seats are arranged in 44 rows, and there are an equal number of seats in each row. How many seats are in each row?

   A   20

   B   22

   C   28

   D   Not Here

2. Allen had 138 pictures. He put 6 pictures on each page of an album. How many pages did he use?

   A   22

   B   23

   C   24

   D   Not Here

3. A store needs to order 144 calculators for a back-to-school sale. The store owner orders the calculators by the case. If 24 calculators come in each case, how many cases does the store owner need?

   A   12

   B   8

   C   6

   D   Not Here

4. Mrs. Akins baked 192 cookies for her 8 grandchildren to take home. If she told her grandchildren to divide the cookies equally among themselves, how many cookies should each child take home?

   A   18

   B   22

   C   23

   D   Not Here

5. A pet store received a shipment of 420 fish. The manager separated the fish equally into 10 tanks. How many fish did the manager put in each tank?

   A   44

   B   42

   C   40

   D   Not Here

Numbers, Operations, and Quantitative Reasoning

Expectation: Use division to solve problems involving whole numbers (no more than 2-digit divisors and 3-digit dividends without technology)

1. Ms. Rashad needs 624 cans of soft drinks for a school party. Each case of soft drinks holds 24 cans. How many cases does Ms. Rashad need to order?

   A   22

   B   26

   C   32

   D   Not Here

2. A school cafeteria holds 216 people. Only 8 people can sit at each table. How many tables are there?

   A   30

   B   28

   C   27

   D   Not Here

3. Hamida hired 18 workers to plant trees on her company's property. Each worker planted the same number of trees. At the end of the day, they had planted a total of 216 trees. How many trees did each worker plant?

   A   12

   B   14

   C   16

   D   Not Here

4. Lizzie knows how to make small puppets from drinking straws. She uses 9 straws for each puppet. How many complete puppets can Lizzie make with a box of 208 straws?

   A   24

   B   23

   C   22

   D   Not Here

5. A bag of candy has 224 pieces. If 14 children share the candy equally, how many pieces of candy will each child have?

   A   12

   B   14

   C   16

   D   Not Here

Numbers, Operations, and Quantitative Reasoning

Expectation: Use division to solve problems involving whole numbers (no more than 2-digit divisors and 3-digit dividends without technology)

1. Mrs. Salas is a florist. She received a shipment of 324 roses and arranged them in bouquets of 12. How many bouquets was she able to make?

   A 28

   B 27

   C 24

   D Not Here

2. A sales clerk must put 4 books in each slot of a book rack. If there are 196 books to place on the book rack, how many slots can the sales clerk fill?

   A 49

   B 48

   C 44

   D Not Here

3. A restaurant owner wants to pay his 20 workers a bonus. He has $500 to give to them. If each worker gets the same amount, how much will each bonus be?

   A $15

   B $24

   C $25

   D Not Here

4. Mr. Falcon has 15 grandchildren. If he gives them $75 to share equally, how much money can each grandchild have?

   A $5

   B $10

   C $15

   D Not Here

5. A baker made 375 chocolate cupcakes and packaged them in 25 boxes. If the baker put an equal number in each box, how many cupcakes were in each box?

   A 20

   B 19

   C 16

   D Not Here

Numbers, Operations, and Quantitative Reasoning

Expectation: Use division to solve problems involving whole numbers (no more than 2-digit divisors and 3-digit dividends without technology)

1. A band has 288 members. During band class, the band members sit in rows of chairs. There are 12 chairs in each row. How many rows of chairs are there?

   A 26

   B 24

   C 22

   D Not Here

2. For a class play, 7 costumes must have an equal number of beads sewn on them. The teacher has 175 beads. If 3 parents help the teacher, how many beads will go on each costume?

   A 58

   B 28

   C 25

   D Not Here

3. An auditorium has 648 seats. The seats are arranged in 12 sections, and each section has the same number of seats. How many seats are in each section?

   A 48

   B 52

   C 53

   D Not Here

4. For a banquet, Mr. Klein wants to put a vase of flowers on each table. He has 126 flowers. If he puts 9 flowers in each vase, how many tables can he decorate with flowers?

   A 14

   B 13

   C 11

   D Not Here

5. Ms. Reinhart needs 234 pencils for students in her art classes. At the store, each box of pencils holds 18 pencils. How many boxes of pencils does Ms. Reinhart need?

   A 12

   B 13

   C 14

   D Not Here

1. Which expression is equal to 24?

   A $2 \times 2 \times 3$

   B $2 \times 3 \times 3$

   C $2 \times 2 \times 2 \times 3$

   D $2 \times 3 \times 3 \times 3$

2. Which set of numbers shows common factors of 18 and 24?

   A 2, 3

   B 2, 4

   C 2, 8

   D 2, 9

3. Which set of numbers shows common factors of 30 and 36?

   A 2, 5

   B 2, 6

   C 2, 8

   D 4, 6

4. Which expression shows the prime factors of 16?

   A $2 \times 2 \times 2$

   B $2 \times 2 \times 3$

   C $2 \times 2 \times 2 \times 2$

   D $2 \times 3 \times 3$

5. Which expression shows the prime factors of 28?

   A $2 \times 2 \times 2 \times 3$

   B $2 \times 3 \times 3$

   C $2 \times 2 \times 7$

   D $2 \times 2 \times 3 \times 3$

6. Which expression shows the prime factors of 30?

   A $3 \times 3 \times 3$

   B $3 \times 3 \times 5$

   C $2 \times 3 \times 3$

   D $2 \times 3 \times 5$

1. Which set of numbers shows common factors of 16 and 28?

   A 2, 4

   B 2, 8

   C 3, 4

   D 4, 7

2. Which expression shows the prime factors of 27?

   A 1×27

   B $1 \times 3 \times 3$

   C 3×9

   D $3 \times 3 \times 3$

3. Which expression shows the prime factors of 54?

   A 2×27

   B 3×6

   C 6×9

   D $2 \times 3 \times 3 \times 3$

4. Which set of numbers shows common factors of 12 and 32?

   A 2, 3

   B 2, 4

   C 4, 6

   D 4, 8

5. Which expression shows the prime factors of 24?

   A $2 \times 2 \times 2$

   B $2 \times 2 \times 3$

   C $2 \times 2 \times 2 \times 3$

   D $2 \times 2 \times 3 \times 5$

6. Which expression shows the prime factors of 72?

   A $2 \times 2 \times 2 \times 2 \times 2$

   B $2 \times 2 \times 3 \times 3 \times 3$

   C $2 \times 2 \times 2 \times 2 \times 3$

   D $2 \times 2 \times 2 \times 3 \times 3$

Objective 1
Exercise 31

Numbers, Operations, and Quantitative Reasoning
Expectation: Identify prime factors of a whole number and common factors of a set of whole numbers

1. Which set of numbers shows common factors of 27 and 36?

   A 3, 4
   B 3, 9
   C 4, 9
   D 6, 9

2. Which expression shows the prime factors of 45?

   A $3 \times 3 \times 3$
   B $2 \times 3 \times 3$
   C $3 \times 3 \times 5$
   D $2 \times 3 \times 5$

3. Which set of numbers shows common factors of 20 and 36?

   A 4, 5
   B 3, 4
   C 2, 4
   D 2, 3

4. Which expression is equal to 42?

   A $2 \times 3 \times 5$
   B $2 \times 3 \times 7$
   C $3 \times 3 \times 7$
   D $3 \times 3 \times 3 \times 3$

5. Which expression shows the prime factors of 40?

   A $2 \times 2 \times 2 \times 2$
   B $2 \times 2 \times 2 \times 3$
   C $2 \times 2 \times 2 \times 5$
   D $2 \times 2 \times 3 \times 5$

6. Which expression shows the prime factors of 32?

   A $2 \times 2 \times 4 \times 4$
   B $2 \times 2 \times 2 \times 4$
   C $2 \times 2 \times 2 \times 2 \times 2$
   D $2 \times 2 \times 2 \times 2 \times 3$

Numbers, Operations, and Quantitative Reasoning

Expectation: Model and record addition and subtraction of fractions with like denominators in problem-solving situations

1. Jackie had 8 quarters, as shown below.

   Jackie spent 2 quarters each day on Monday, Wednesday, and Friday. What fraction of the quarters does she have left?

   A $\frac{1}{8}$

   B $\frac{2}{8}$

   C $\frac{4}{8}$

   D $\frac{6}{8}$

2. Peter had 1 dozen cans of soda (12 cans). Four friends visited his house and drank 1 can of soda each. Peter drank 2 cans of soda. What fraction of the cans of soda is left?

   A $\frac{6}{12}$

   B $\frac{8}{12}$

   C $\frac{10}{12}$

   D $\frac{12}{12}$

3. Parker had a bag of 14 pieces of candy. Parker ate 2 pieces and 3 of his friends ate 3 pieces each. What fraction of the candies was eaten?

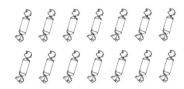

   A $\frac{2}{14}$

   B $\frac{3}{14}$

   C $\frac{9}{14}$

   D $\frac{11}{14}$

4. Together, Dante and Diane had 9 quarters. Dante spent 3 quarters on a bag of chips. Diane spent 4 quarters on a hot dog. What fraction of the quarters did they spend?

   A $\frac{7}{9}$

   B $\frac{4}{9}$

   C $\frac{3}{9}$

   D $\frac{7}{18}$

Objective 1
Exercise 33

Numbers, Operations, and Quantitative Reasoning

Expectation: Model and record addition and subtraction of fractions with like denominators in problem-solving situations

1. Jacob has 10 notebooks on his shelf. He uses 1 for writing, 1 for Spanish, 1 for science, 2 for math, 1 for history, and 1 for reading. What fraction of the notebooks is **NOT** used?

   A $\frac{2}{10}$

   B $\frac{3}{10}$

   C $\frac{7}{10}$

   D $\frac{8}{10}$

2. Mr. Robert's fifth-grade class drew maps for social studies. He gave the class a box of 32 colored pencils for the project. Group A used 6 pencils, group B used 4 pencils, group C used 8 pencils, and group D used 5 pencils. What fraction of the pencils was used?

   A $\frac{4}{32}$

   B $\frac{5}{32}$

   C $\frac{9}{32}$

   D $\frac{23}{32}$

3. This weekend, Sal opened a lemonade stand. She had a bag of 24 plastic cups for serving lemonade. On Friday, she sold 12 cups of lemonade. On Saturday, it rained, so she sold 0 cups. On Sunday, she sold 8 cups. Which fraction of the cups does she have left?

   A $\frac{20}{24}$

   B $\frac{12}{24}$

   C $\frac{6}{24}$

   D $\frac{4}{24}$

4. Ms. Jackson's fifth-grade class is having a pizza party. She orders 18 pizzas. Three are pepperoni, 4 are sausage, and the remaining pizzas are cheese. What fraction of the pizzas is **NOT** cheese?

   A $\frac{3}{18}$

   B $\frac{4}{18}$

   C $\frac{7}{18}$

   D $\frac{11}{18}$

Objective 1
Exercise 34

Numbers, Operations, and Quantitative Reasoning

Expectation: Model and record addition and subtraction of fractions with like denominators in problem-solving situations

1. Oscar had 15 small fish. He brought the fish to school and gave some to his classmates. Three girls and 1 boy took 2 fish each. What fraction of the fish was left?

A $\frac{2}{15}$

B $\frac{7}{15}$

C $\frac{8}{15}$

D $\frac{12}{15}$

2. Samantha had 20 dog treats for her dog, Skippy. Every time Skippy did a trick correctly, he got a treat. On Monday, Skippy did 2 tricks correctly. On Tuesday, he did 3 tricks correctly. On Wednesday, he did 6 tricks correctly. What fraction of treats does Samantha have left to give Skippy?

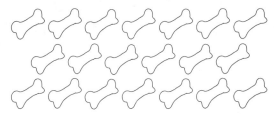

A $\frac{2}{20}$

B $\frac{6}{20}$

C $\frac{9}{20}$

D $\frac{11}{20}$

3. Ms. Joseph brought 21 jars of paint for the students in her art class to use. Group 1 used 8 jars. Group 2 used 6 jars. Group 3 used 7 jars. What fraction of the jars of paint did group 1 and group 3 use?

A $\frac{18}{21}$

B $\frac{15}{21}$

C $\frac{14}{21}$

D $\frac{15}{42}$

4. Anna and her sister had 6 lollipops. Anna ate 3 lollipops. Her sister ate 2 lollipops. Anna lost 1 lollipop on the school bus. What fraction of the lollipops did Anna and her sister eat?

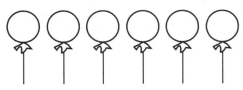

A $\frac{5}{6}$

B $\frac{3}{6}$

C $\frac{2}{6}$

D $\frac{1}{6}$

1. Sarina bought 4 items at a jewelry store. The least expensive item was $4.95. The most expensive item was $14.95. Before tax is added, what is a **reasonable** range for the total cost of the items?

    A   Less than $10

    B   Between $15 and $20

    C   Between $30 and $45

    D   More than $60

2. Carl watches television from 90 to 120 minutes a day, 5 days a week. Which is a **reasonable** total of the number of minutes he watches television in 2 weeks?

    A   1,000 min

    B   600 min

    C   500 min

    D   350 min

3. Mr. Jones painted the outside of his house. He used from 4.5 to 7 liters of paint on each wall. Which is a **reasonable** total of the amount of paint he used on the 10 walls of his house?

    A   40 L

    B   60 L

    C   80 L

    D   100 L

4. A chef uses from 7 to 10 cups of flour in each loaf of French bread that she makes. Which is a **reasonable** total of the amount of flour the chef would use to make 30 loaves of French bread?

    A   150 c

    B   250 c

    C   350 c

    D   450 c

Numbers, Operations, and Quantitative Reasoning

Expectation: Round whole numbers and decimals through tenths to approximate reasonable results in problem situations

1. Mrs. Thomas made 12 costumes for the school play. She spent from 3 to 5 hours on each costume. Which is a **reasonable** amount of time for Mrs. Thomas to have spent making the 12 costumes?

   A 30 hr
   B 55 hr
   C 75 hr
   D 80 hr

2. Michelle bought 5 gifts for her cousins who live in Waco. The least expensive gift was $4.50, and the most expensive gift was $6.50. Before adding tax, what is a **reasonable** range for the total cost of the gifts Michelle bought?

   A More than $60
   B Between $50 and $60
   C Between $40 and $50
   D Less than $30

3. Last week, Tony took 5 math quizzes. His lowest score was 78 and his highest score was 92. Which is a **reasonable** total of all 5 quiz scores?

   A 500 points
   B 400 points
   C 350 points
   D 300 points

4. An electronics store had 5 customers in the morning. Each customer bought something. The lowest sale was $55, and the highest sale was $75. What is a **reasonable** range for the total of the 5 sales?

   A Less than $200
   B Between $220 and $280
   C Between $320 and $350
   D More than $400

Objective 1
Exercise 38

Numbers, Operations, and Quantitative Reasoning

Expectation: Round whole numbers and decimals through tenths to approximate reasonable results in problem situations

1. Each student in Mr. Marlin's class earned from 45 to 60 points to spend in the classroom store. If there are 20 students in Mr. Marlin's class, which is a **reasonable** total of the number of points earned by all the students?

   A 2,000 points
   B 1,500 points
   C 1,000 points
   D 800 points

2. A post office receives from 900 to 1,200 letters 6 days of the week. What is a **reasonable** range for the total number of letters the post office receives in 2 weeks?

   A Less than 8,000 letters
   B Between 8,000 and 10,000 letters
   C Between 10,000 and 14,000 letters
   D More than 14,000 letters

3. A janitor cleans 5 classrooms each day. The most time he spends cleaning a room is 45 minutes, and the least time he spends is 30 minutes. What is a **reasonable** range for the total amount of time the janitor spends cleaning the 5 classrooms?

   A Less than 90 minutes
   B Between 90 and 120 minutes
   C Between 120 and 150 minutes
   D More than 150 minutes

4. A store counted the number of shoppers who entered the store during a 4-hour period. The greatest number of shoppers who entered during 1 hour was 100, and the fewest number was 80. What is a **reasonable** range for the total number of shoppers who entered during the 4 hours?

   A Less than 280 shoppers
   B Between 280 and 320 shoppers
   C Between 320 and 360 shoppers
   D More than 400 shoppers

1. Vanessa is making 5 wall hangings for a craft show. Each wall hanging will have a trim made of ribbon. The longest piece of ribbon is 18.8 inches, and the shortest piece of ribbon is 10.2 inches. What is a **reasonable** range for the total amount of ribbon Vanessa will need for the wall hangings?

   A   More than 100 inches

   B   Between 50 and 90 inches

   C   Between 30 and 50 inches

   D   Less than 30 inches

2. Craig's team played 10 basketball games. The team's highest score was 44 points. The team's lowest score was 38 points. Which is a **reasonable** total of all 10 game scores?

   A   400 points

   B   300 points

   C   250 points

   D   200 points

3. On her way from San Antonio to El Paso, Mrs. Keller drove between 60 and 70 miles per hour. The distance from San Antonio to El Paso is 550 miles. What is a **reasonable** range for the total number of hours Mrs. Keller drove?

   A   More than 10 hours

   B   Between 8 and 9 hours

   C   Between 6 and 7 hours

   D   Less than 6 hours

4. An athlete runs 5 days a week. The longest distance she runs in 1 day is 7 kilometers. The shortest distance she runs in 1 day is 5 kilometers. Which is a **reasonable** total for the distance the athlete runs in 10 days?

   A   30 km

   B   60 km

   C   80 km

   D   120 km

1. Eleanor bought a sweater for $18.99, a skirt for $9.99, and a pair of shoes for $29.99. Which is the **best estimate** for how much she spent on her clothes?

   A $40

   B $50

   C $60

   D $70

2. A band performed 3 concerts. At the first concert, 412 people attended. At the second concert, 594 people attended. At the third concert, 382 people attended. Which is the **best estimate** for the total number of people who attended the 3 concerts?

   A 1,100

   B 1,200

   C 1,300

   D 1,400

3. Christopher had $285 for school clothes. He spent $21.85 for shoes and $11.15 for a shirt. Which is the **best estimate** for the amount of money Christopher had left after buying the shoes and shirt?

   A $330

   B $270

   C $220

   D $200

4. Mr. Evans bought 10 books. The most expensive book cost $5.95, and the least expensive book cost $2.95. Which is the **best estimate** for the total amount Mr. Evans spent on the books?

   A Less than $20

   B Between $20 and $30

   C Between $30 and $50

   D More than $60

5. There are 32 packs of gum in a box. Which is the **best estimate** for the number of packs in 18 boxes?

   A 400

   B 500

   C 600

   D 700

6. A bag holds 1,996 small pieces of gum. Mrs. Walters has 21 students in her class and wants to divide the gum equally among them. Which is the **best estimate** for the number of pieces of gum each student will get?

   A 80

   B 100

   C 120

   D 200

1. Ribbon costs $1.99 per yard at a craft store. Melanie needs 21 yards of ribbon. Which is the **best estimate** for the cost of the ribbon Melanie will buy?

   A $10
   B $20
   C $30
   D $40

2. Scott mows lawns and runs errands to earn spending money. Last year, he earned $287 mowing lawns and $112 running errands. Which is the **best estimate** of the total amount Scott made last year?

   A $500
   B $400
   C $300
   D $200

3. Two football teams, the Lions and the Rams, played in a stadium that has 22,184 seats. Lions fans bought 8,892 tickets. Rams fans bought the rest of the tickets. Which is the **best estimate** for the number of tickets the Rams fans bought?

   A 9,000
   B 10,000
   C 12,000
   D 13,000

4. A department store had a 3-day sale. On the first day, there were 1,819 shoppers. On the second day, there were 1,310 shoppers. On the third day, there were 2,940 shoppers. Which is the **best estimate** for the total number of shoppers at the sale?

   A 4,800
   B 5,200
   C 6,000
   D 8,000

5. Each month, Paula's dog eats a full bag of dog food that weighs 28 pounds. Which is the **best estimate** of the amount of dog food Paula's dog eats in 1 year (12 months)?

   A 150 lb
   B 200 lb
   C 300 lb
   D 400 lb

6. A clerk had 2,900 bonus bags to give away during a store's grand opening. If the clerk gives away about 490 bags an hour, which is the **best estimate** of how long it will take her to give away all the bags?

   A 6 hr
   B 5 hr
   C 4 hr
   D 3 hr

1. Rodney spent $39.89 on a jacket, $19.49 on shoes, and $17.90 on a shirt. What is the **best estimate** of how much Rodney spent before tax?

   A More than $90

   B Between $80 and $90

   C Between $70 and $80

   D Less than $70

2. A large amusement park has 3 outdoor theaters. The first theater seats 1,200 people. The second theater seats 1,050. The third seats 1,700. Which is the **best estimate** for the total number of seats at the 3 theaters?

   A 3,000

   B 4,000

   C 5,000

   D 6,000

3. Cheri wants to buy a new TV for her family. The TV costs $488. Cheri has $175 in her savings account and $27 in cash. Which is the **best estimate** for how much more money she needs in order to buy the TV?

   A $100

   B $200

   C $300

   D $400

4. Kari walks for exercise. In May, she walked 29.9 kilometers. In June, she walked 31.6 kilometers. In July, she walked 27.3 kilometers. Which is the **best estimate** for the total distance she walked in the 3 months?

   A 60 km

   B 70 km

   C 80 km

   D 90 km

5. The distance between San Antonio and Austin is about 79 miles. Mary drove from San Antonio to Austin and then back to San Antonio each day for 5 days. Which is the **best estimate** of the total distance she traveled during the 5 days?

   A 800 mi

   B 700 mi

   C 500 mi

   D 400 mi

6. Mrs. Grove's car holds 18 gallons of gasoline. She can drive 388 miles with 1 full tank of gasoline. Which is the **best estimate** of how far Mrs. Grove can drive with 1 gallon of gasoline?

   A 30 mi

   B 20 mi

   C 15 mi

   D 10 mi

Objective 2

Patterns, Relationships, and Algebraic Reasoning

A. Use pictures to make generalizations about determining all possible combinations

B. Use lists, tables, charts, and diagrams to find patterns and make generalizations, such as a procedure for determining equivalent fractions

C. Identify prime and composite numbers using models and patterns in factor pairs

D. Select from and use diagrams and number sentences to represent real-life situations

Objective 2
Exercise 1

Patterns, Relationships, and Algebraic Reasoning
Expectation: Use pictures to make generalizations about determining all possible combinations

1. Tommy's baby brother is stacking and unstacking blocks. The picture shows the blocks he used.

   In how many different arrangements can the blocks be stacked if 3 blocks are used in each arrangement?

   A 4
   B 6
   C 16
   D 24

2. Lily has 3 scarves, 2 belts, and 2 pins. If she wears 1 of each item, how many different combinations can she make?

Scarves	Belts	Pins

   A 5
   B 7
   C 10
   D 12

3. At lunch, students may choose from among 3 main dishes, 2 salads, and 3 vegetables. How many different lunches can students have if they choose 1 item from each group?

   A 8
   B 12
   C 18
   D 20

4. Mr. Marcus is buying a new car. He can choose from the features listed below.

Color	Doors	Other
Blue	2	Radio
Silver	4	CD/Tape Player
Black		

   If he chooses 1 feature from each column, how many different combinations of features can he choose?

   A 6
   B 7
   C 12
   D 20

5. Cindy, Marty, Kami, and Dawn were on a relay team. For a race, they had to stand in line, one behind the other. In how many different ways could the girls arrange themselves in line?

   A 4
   B 8
   C 12
   D 24

**Objective 2
Exercise 2**

Patterns, Relationships, and Algebraic Reasoning
Expectation: Use pictures to make generalizations about determining all possible combinations

1. At a luncheon, the guests are allowed to make their own sandwiches. The chart shows the items they could choose.

Sandwich Items	
Ham	
Cheese	
Pickles	
Tomato	

If a guest chooses 2 items, how many different sandwiches can be made?

A 6

B 8

C 12

D 24

2. Gretchen is ordering an ice-cream sundae. She may choose from the toppings listed below.

Syrup	Sprinkles
Hot Fudge	Peanuts
Caramel	Chocolate Chips
Cherry	Peppermint Bites
Strawberry	

If she orders 1 topping from each column, how many different sundaes can she order?

A 15

B 12

C 7

D 4

3. Bonnie has 5 different baseball pennants to hang on her bedroom wall. If she places them in a straight row on the wall, how many different arrangements can she make?

Record your answer and fill in the bubbles on your answer document. Be sure to use the correct place value.

			.
⓪	⓪	⓪	
①	①	①	
②	②	②	
③	③	③	
④	④	④	
⑤	⑤	⑤	
⑥	⑥	⑥	
⑦	⑦	⑦	
⑧	⑧	⑧	
⑨	⑨	⑨	

4. Doug is playing with a model train set. The picture shows the train cars he has.

In how many different ways can he arrange the passenger cars on the track?

A 30

B 24

C 12

D 8

5. Mona's grandmother keeps a treasure box for her grandchildren. The box has 4 different games, 5 kinds of stickers, and 2 kinds of candy. If Mona selects 1 of each item, how many different combinations can she make?

A 11

B 20

C 30

D 40

Objective 2
Exercise 3

Patterns, Relationships, and Algebraic Reasoning
Expectation: Use pictures to make generalizations about determining all possible combinations

1. Mr. Frances has trophies to display in his living room.

   If he places the trophies in 1 line, how many different arrangements can he make?

   A   24
   B   16
   C   6
   D   4

2. Jeannie has 3 sets of colored socks, 2 blouses, and 5 hair ribbons. If she selects 1 item from each group, how many different outfits can she make?

   A   30
   B   25
   C   15
   D   8

3. The students in Mrs. Clark's class made ice-cream sundaes. There were 3 kinds of ice cream, 3 kinds of syrup, and 3 kinds of toppings. If the students could choose 1 item from each group, how many different kinds of sundaes could they make?

   A   9
   B   15
   C   18
   D   27

4. Clay bought the clothes listed below.

Shirts	Pants	Shoes
White	Blue	Black
Blue	Black	Brown
Green	Khaki	

   If he wears 1 item from each column, how many different outfits can he make?

   A   8
   B   12
   C   18
   D   24

5. The trucks below are waiting to park at a depot.

   The trucks must enter one at a time and park in a line, each behind another. In how many different ways can the trucks park?

   A   25
   B   60
   C   120
   D   200

1. At a restaurant, customers may choose 1 item from each row in the chart.

Meats	Chicken	Ham	Steak
Vegetables	Peas	Carrots	Beets
Breads	French	White	
Desserts	Apple Pie	Lemon Cake	

How many different meal combinations can a customer make from the choices?

A 42

B 36

C 24

D 16

2. Cheryl, Marie, Laurel, and Ally want to have a picture taken together. If they sit side by side in 1 row, in how many different arrangements could the girls sit?

A 4

B 6

C 16

D 24

3. At a party, guests could choose from 3 salads, 2 main dishes, 2 vegetables, and 2 desserts. If each guest took 1 item from each group, how many different meal combinations could be made?

A 9

B 14

C 20

D 24

4. Alice has some new charms for her bracelet.

The charms can be arranged in any order. In how many different ways can Alice arrange the charms?

A 14

B 25

C 60

D 120

5. At Adams Elementary School, the students wear uniforms. The boys must wear pants, a shirt, and a sweater chosen from the uniform list below.

Pants	Shirts	Sweaters
Blue (long)	White	Blue
Black (long)	Blue	Black
Blue (shorts)		Blue (vest)

How many different outfits can the boys make from the choices?

A 8

B 10

C 18

D 24

Patterns, Relationships, and Algebraic Reasoning

Expectation: Use lists, tables, charts, and diagrams to find patterns and make generalizations, such as a procedure for determining equivalent fractions

1. Look at the pattern of shaded boxes in the number chart below.

1	2	3	4	5
6	7	8	9	10
11	12	13	14	15
16	17	18	19	20
21	22	23	24	25

Which box should be shaded in order to complete the pattern correctly?

A 22

B 21

C 15

D 10

2. Janie bought 30 candies to give to her friends. At the end of 1 hour, Janie had 26 candies left. At the end of 2 hours, she had 22 candies left. At the end of 3 hours, she had 18 candies left. If she continued the pattern, how many candies did Janie have left at the end of **5** hours?

A 26

B 20

C 14

D 10

3. A magician performed a trick with scarves. He waved his wand once, and there were 4 scarves. He waved his wand a second time, and there were 8 scarves. He waved his wand a third time, and there were 16 scarves. If he continued the pattern, how many scarves were there after he waved his wand the **fifth** time?

Record your answer and fill in the bubbles on your answer document. Be sure to use the correct place value.

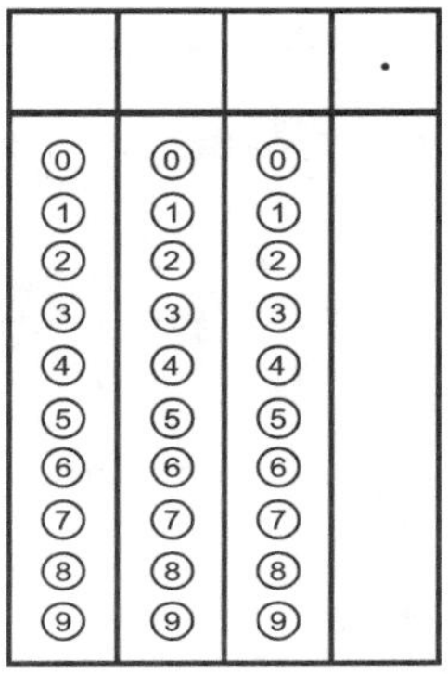

4. Look at the pattern of shaded boxes in the number chart below.

31	32	33	34	35
36	37	38	39	40
41	42	43	44	45
46	47	48	49	50
51	52	53	54	55

Which box does **NOT** fit the pattern and should **NOT** be shaded?

A 37

B 43

C 45

D 55

Patterns, Relationships, and Algebraic Reasoning

Expectation: Use lists, tables, charts, and diagrams to find patterns and make generalizations, such as a procedure for determining equivalent fractions

1. Look at the pattern of expressions listed in the chart below.

    $$2 \times 2 = 2^2$$
    $$2 \times 2 \times 2 = 2^3$$
    $$2 \times 2 \times 2 \times 2 = 2^4$$
    $$2 \times 2 \times 2 \times 2 \times 2 = 2^5$$
    $$\underline{\hspace{4cm}} = 2^6$$

    Which expression goes in the blank space?

    A $2 \times 2 \times 2$

    B 2×2

    C 2×26

    D $2 \times 2 \times 2 \times 2 \times 2 \times 2$

2. Some fifth-grade students painted flowers on a mural. The chart shows how many flowers they painted in each section of the mural.

Section	Daisies	Sunflowers
1	2	4
2	3	8
3	4	12
4		

    If the students continued the pattern, how many sunflowers did they paint in the **fourth** section?

    A 18

    B 16

    C 14

    D 5

3. The chart shows how many teacher assistants are needed to work at a summer camp.

Number of Campers	Number of Assistants
40	6
80	12
120	18
160	
200	

    How many assistants are needed to work with **200** campers?

    A 20

    B 28

    C 30

    D 32

4. A marching band performed on a football field. There were 5 members in the first row, 8 members in the second row, 12 members in the third row, and 17 members in the fourth row. If the pattern continued, how many members were in the **sixth** row?

    A 20

    B 23

    C 24

    D 30

Patterns, Relationships, and Algebraic Reasoning

Expectation: Use lists, tables, charts, and diagrams to find patterns and make generalizations, such as a procedure for determining equivalent fractions

1. Aaron bought 3 sets of colored pencils. Each set had 8 pencils and cost $4.50. Which method could Aaron use to find the total cost of all 3 sets?

    A   Multiply $4.50 by 8

    B   Divide $4.50 by 3

    C   Add 3 and 8, then multiply by $4.50

    D   Multiply $4.50 times 3

2. The sign shows the rates charged to enter an amusement park.

    # Fun-O-Rama Park

    Adults: $10.50

    Children: $7.50 (ages 12 and under)

    Family Packs
    2 Adults and 2 Children: $32.00
    2 Adults and 3 Children: $38.00

    Mr. and Mrs. Jamison are going to the park with their 3 children, ages 10, 12, and 13. What is the lowest price they can pay to enter the park?

    A $38.00

    B $39.50

    C $42.50

    D $46.50

3. Mickey and 2 friends went walking on 3 evenings. The first evening, they walked 2 miles; the second evening, they walked 2.5 miles; and the third evening, they walked 2.8 miles. Which method could be used to find the total number of miles Mickey walked?

    A   Add 2 and 2.5, then multiply by 3

    B   Multiply 2 by 3, then add 2.8

    C   Add 2.8 and 2.5 and 2

    D   Add 2, 2.5, and 2.8, then divide by 3

4. The fifth grade is going on a field trip to the museum. The school district has 14 vans that can be used on the trip. At least 8 adults and 84 students will attend the field trip. Only 8 passengers can fit in each van. What is the fewest number of vans that can be used?

    A   13

    B   12

    C   11

    D   10

Patterns, Relationships, and Algebraic Reasoning

Expectation: Use lists, tables, charts, and diagrams to find patterns and make generalizations, such as a procedure for determining equivalent fractions

1. The table shows the rates for using the exercise machines at a gym.

Rates for Exercise Machines

Plan 1	Plan 2
$20 per month for 10 hours $1.50 for each additional hour	$40 per month Unlimited hours

Alicia wants to decide which plan would be less expensive for her. What additional information should she use to make her decision?

A The number of her friends who go to the gym

B Which machines she likes to use

C The number of people who use Plan 2

D The number of hours she plans to spend at the gym

2. During a 10-day bicycle trip, Shawn rode 540 miles. During the same 10-day trip, Karina rode 485 miles. Which method could be used to find how much farther Shawn rode than Karina?

A Add 540 and 485

B Subtract 485 from 540

C Add 540 and 485, then divide by 10

D Subtract 485 from 540, then multiply by 10

3. The chart shows how many envelopes workers can seal in 1 hour.

Envelopes Sealed in 1 Hour	Number of Workers
1,000	4
2,000	8
3,000	12
4,000	16
5,000	20

Based on the information in the chart, about how many envelopes can 1 worker seal in 1 hour?

A 100

B 150

C 200

D 250

4. Mrs. King made 4 batches of cookies for the 24 students in her class. Each student received 3 cookies. Which method could be used to find the total number of cookies all the students received?

A Multiply 4 by 3 by 24

B Divide 24 by 4, then multiply by 3

C Multiply 24 by 3

D Multiply 24 by 4

1. Which group names all the whole number factors of a composite number?

   A   1, 13
   B   1, 2, 9
   C   1, 2, 4, 8, 16
   D   1, 2, 5, 6

2. Which figure best represents a prime number?

   A

   B

   C

   D

3. Which of the following is **NOT** a prime number?

   A   2
   B   3
   C   5
   D   9

4. Which group names all the whole number factors of a composite number?

   A   1, 2, 3, 6, 9, 18
   B   1, 19
   C   1, 2, 3, 8, 16
   D   1, 6, 9

5. Which array of stars best represents a prime number?

   A   ☆ ☆ ☆ ☆ ☆
       ☆ ☆ ☆ ☆ ☆ ☆

   B   ☆ ☆ ☆ ☆ ☆ ☆ ☆ ☆

   C   ☆ ☆ ☆ ☆ ☆ ☆ ☆
       ☆ ☆ ☆ ☆ ☆ ☆ ☆

   D   ☆ ☆ ☆ ☆ ☆
       ☆ ☆ ☆ ☆ ☆

1. Which group names all the whole number factors of a composite number?

   A 2, 3, 12, 24
   B 1, 5, 10
   C 1, 3, 5, 15
   D 1, 31

2. Which array of stars best represents a composite number?

   A ✺✺✺✺✺
      ✺✺✺✺✺

   B ✺✺✺✺✺✺✺

   C ✺✺✺✺✺✺✺✺✺✺✺

   D ✺✺✺✺✺

3. Which of the following is **NOT** a prime number?

   A 17
   B 19
   C 37
   D 45

4. Which group names all the whole number factors of a prime number?

   A 1, 6
   B 1, 7
   C 1, 2, 3
   D 1, 2, 3, 5

5. On which chart are 2 prime numbers in shaded boxes?

A
1	2	3	4	5
6	7	8	9	10
11	12	13	14	15
16	17	18	19	20
21	22	23	24	25

(shaded: 3, 15)

B
1	2	3	4	5
6	7	8	9	10
11	12	13	14	15
16	17	18	19	20
21	22	23	24	25

(shaded: 5, 9)

C
1	2	3	4	5
6	7	8	9	10
11	12	13	14	15
16	17	18	19	20
21	22	23	24	25

(shaded: 3, 17)

D
1	2	3	4	5
6	7	8	9	10
11	12	13	14	15
16	17	18	19	20
21	22	23	24	25

(shaded: 12, 18)

1. Which group names all the whole number factors of a composite number?

   A   1, 2, 6, 7
   B   1, 3, 9, 27
   C   1, 3, 6, 9
   D   1, 5

2. Which array of stars best represents a prime number?

   A   ✳ ✳ ✳ ✳ ✳

   B   ✳ ✳ ✳ ✳
       ✳ ✳ ✳ ✳

   C   ✳ ✳ ✳ ✳ ✳ ✳
       ✳ ✳ ✳ ✳ ✳ ✳

   D   ✳ ✳ ✳ ✳ ✳
       ✳ ✳ ✳ ✳

3. Which of the following is **NOT** a composite number?

   A   22
   B   27
   C   38
   D   41

4. Which group names all the whole number factors of a prime number?

   A   1, 2, 3, 6
   B   1, 17
   C   1, 2, 3, 4, 6, 12
   D   1, 3, 7, 21

5. Which of the following is **NOT** a prime number?

   A   17
   B   23
   C   32
   D   43

Expectation: Identify prime and composite numbers using models and patterns in factor pairs

1. Which group names all the whole number factors of a prime number?

A 1, 2, 4, 7

B 1, 3, 9, 27

C 1, 3, 6

D 1, 3

2. Which array of hearts best represents a prime number?

A 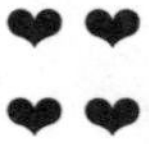

B 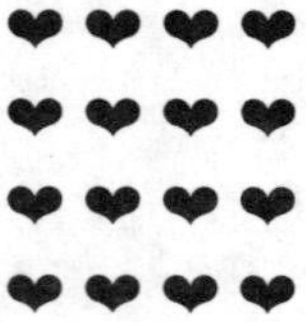

C 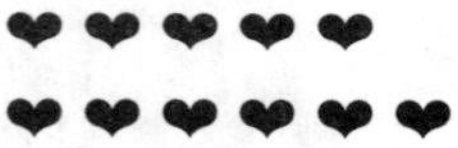

D 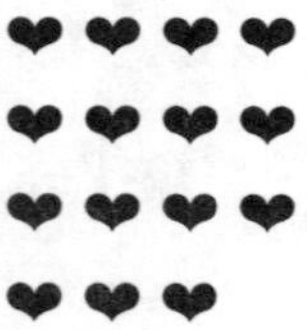

3. Which of the following is **NOT** a composite number?

A 14

B 23

C 34

D 38

4. Which group names all the whole number factors of a composite number?

A 1, 3, 11, 33

B 1, 13

C 1, 2, 6, 12

D 1, 2, 14, 28

5. Look at the number chart below.

1	2	3	4	5
6	7	8	9	10
11	12	13	14	15
16	17	18	19	20
21	22	23	24	25

How many prime numbers are in shaded boxes?

A 7

B 6

C 4

D 1

1. Deborah is shopping for paper for her scrapbook. Each package of white paper has 10 sheets. Deborah needs 3 packages of white paper. Colored paper is sold by the sheet. Deborah needs 5 sheets of colored paper to make page dividers. Which number sentence could be used to find T, the total number of sheets of paper Deborah needs to buy.

   A $T = (10 \times 3) + (10 \times 5)$

   B $T = (10 \times 3) + 5$

   C $T = (5 \times 3) + 10$

   D $T = (10 \times 3) - 5$

2. Shane baked 6 cakes for the school bake sale. He used 2 cups of sugar and 3 cups of flour in each cake. Which number sentence could be used to find the total number of cups of flour Shane used in the cakes?

   A $(6 + 2) \times 3 = \square$

   B $6 \times (2 + 3) = \square$

   C $6 \times 3 = \square$

   D $(6 \times 3) \div \square = 3$

3. At Washington Elementary School, there are 4 morning classes. Each of the first 3 classes lasts 45 minutes. The fourth morning class lasts 55 minutes. Which number sentence could be used to find S, the total amount of time the 4 morning classes last?

   A $S = (45 \times 3) + 55$

   B $S = (45 \times 3) - 55$

   C $S = (45 + 55) \times 3$

   D $S = (55 \times 3) + 45$

4. Mrs. Davis took 30 students to the museum. For the museum tour, the guides arranged the students in 3 equal groups. Two adults went with each student group. Which number sentence could be used to find the total number of people in each tour group?

   A $30 + 3 + 2 = \square$

   B $(30 \times 3) \div 2 = \square$

   C $(30 \div 3) + 2 = \square$

   D $(30 \div 2) + 3 = \square$

1. Shaila works at a grocery store and earns $8 an hour. She receives a $15 bonus each month if she does not miss any days of work. In May, she worked 25 hours and was never absent. Which number sentence could be used to find T, the total amount Shaila earned for the month of May?

   A $T = 25 \times (8 + 15)$
   B $T = (8 \times 25) + 15$
   C $T = (8 \times 25) \div 15$
   D $T = (8 + 15) + 25$

2. Terrence had 120 baseball cards. His brother Eddie had 100 baseball cards. Terrence gave half of his baseball cards to Eddie. Then, he gave 10 more cards to his best friend. Which number sentence could be used to find the total number of baseball cards Terrence has left?

   A $(120 \times 2) - 10 = \square$
   B $(120 - 10) \div 2 = \square$
   C $120 \div 10 = \square$
   D $(120 \div 2) - 10 = \square$

3. Cecilia's family went to a movie. They bought 5 boxes of popcorn at $3.00 per box and 5 drinks at $2.00 per cup. They spent $25 on tickets. Which number sentence could be used to find S, the total amount the family spent on popcorn and drinks?

   A $S = (5 \times 3) + (5 \times 2)$
   B $S = (5 \times 3) + (2 + 25)$
   C $S = 5 + 3 + 2 + 25$
   D $S = 5 \times (2 + 3 + 25)$

4. Marisol made flower arrangements for a party. She had 27 roses and put an equal number of roses in each of 9 vases. Then, she added 3 daisies to each vase. Which number sentence could be used to find the total number of flowers Marisol put in each vase?

   A $(27 \div 9) \times 3 = \square$
   B $(3 \times 27) \div \square = 9$
   C $(27 \div 9) \div 3 = \square$
   D $(27 \div 9) + 3 = \square$

1. Sunita has belonged to a reading club for 2 years. In August, each member of the club paid $10 for dues. Each member also bought 3 books, which cost $6 each. There are 8 people in the club. Which number sentence could be used to find T, the total amount paid by each member of the club in August?

   A $T = (8 \times 10) + (8 \times 6)$
   B $T = (8 \times 10 \times 6)$
   C $T = (2 \times 10) + (3 \times 6)$
   D $T = (6 \times 3) + 10$

2. Mrs. Denver divided a box of 64 crayons among 8 students. Then, she gave each student 2 pieces of drawing paper. Which number sentence could be used to find the total number of crayons each student received?

   A $64 \times 8 = \square$
   B $(64 \div 8) + 2 = \square$
   C $64 \div 8 = \square$
   D $(64 \div \square) - 2 = 8$

3. Emily had $30 to spend at an amusement park. She spent $\frac{1}{3}$ of the money for a ticket to get into the park. She spent $3 for a drink and $5 for a hamburger. Which number sentence could be used to find the amount of money Emily spent?

   A $(30 \times 3) + (3 + 5) = \square$
   B $(30 \div 3) + (3 + 5) = \square$
   C $(30 \div 3) - (3 + 5) = \square$
   D $(30 \div 3) \times (3 + 5) = \square$

4. Hank ordered 4 CDs from his favorite Web site. He spent $16 for each CD and also paid a $5 delivery charge. Which number sentence could be used to find T, the total amount Hank paid for his order?

   A $T = (4 \times 16) + 5$
   B $T = (16 \div 4) + 5$
   C $T = (4 \times 16) \times 5$
   D $T = (5 \times 4) + 16$

1. Jeff wants to build 5 birdhouses as gifts. To build 1 birdhouse, he uses 8 pieces of wood and 48 nails. Which number sentence could be used to find the total number of nails Jeff will need to build the 5 birdhouses?

    A $(5 \times 8) + (5 \times 48) = \square$

    B $5 \times 48 = \square$

    C $(5 \times 48) + 8 = \square$

    D $8 \times 48 \times 5 = \square$

2. Suzanne bought 5 boxes of cookies for her party. Each box had 24 cookies. At the party, her guests ate 75 cookies. Which number sentence could be used to find S, the number of cookies Suzanne had left after the party?

    A $S = (5 \times 24) + 75$

    B $S = 24 + 75$

    C $S = (5 \times 24) - 75$

    D $S = 5 + 24 + 75$

3. The fourth- and fifth-grade students at Red River Elementary are taking a test. There are 154 fourth-grade students and 212 fifth-grade students. Each student needs 2 pencils for the test. Which number sentence could be used to find T, the total number of pencils needed by the fourth- and fifth-grade students?

    A $T = (2 \times 154) + 212$

    B $T = 154 + 212 + 2$

    C $T = (154 + 212) \div 2$

    D $T = 2 \times (154 + 212)$

4. Barbie earned $44 for babysitting and $26 for running errands. She must use half of the money she earned to repay a loan from her mother. Which number sentence could be used to find how much money Barbie owes her mother?

    A $(44 + 26) \div 2 = \square$

    B $(44 - 26) \times 2 = \square$

    C $(44 \times 26) \div 2 = \square$

    D $(44 + 26) \times 2 = \square$

Objective 3

Geometry and Spatial Reasoning

A. Identify critical attributes including parallel, perpendicular, and congruent parts of geometric shapes and solids

B. Use critical attributes to define geometric shapes and solids

C. Sketch the results of translations, rotations, and reflections

D. Describe the transformation that generates 1 figure from the other when given 2 congruent figures

E. Locate and name points on a coordinate grid using ordered pairs of whole numbers

Geometry and Spatial Reasoning

Expectation: Identify critical attributes including parallel, perpendicular, and congruent parts of geometric shapes and solids

1. Which figure is a quadrilateral?

A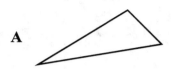

B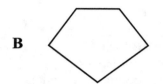

C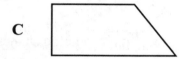

D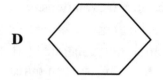

2. Figure ABCD is a parallelogram.

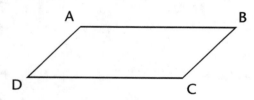

Which statement is true?

A ∠A = ∠C
B ∠A = ∠B
C ∠B = ∠C
D ∠C = ∠D

3. What is the measure of ∠A?

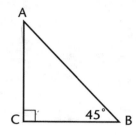

A 90°
B 60°
C 45°
D 30°

4. How many vertices does a cube have?

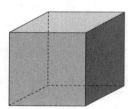

A 12
B 8
C 6
D 4

Geometry and Spatial Reasoning

Expectation: Identify critical attributes including parallel, perpendicular, and congruent parts of geometric shapes and solids

1. Figure ABCDE is a pentagon.

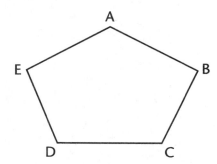

Which statement is true?

A   All angles must be congruent.

B   All sides must be congruent.

C   The figure must have 5 sides and 5 angles.

D $\overline{AB}$ and $\overline{DE}$ must be parallel lines.

2. How many faces does a rectangular pyramid have?

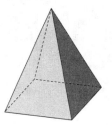

A   3

B   4

C   5

D   6

3. Figure RSTU is a square.

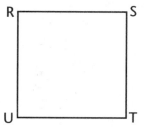

Which statement is true?

A   All angles and sides of figure RSTU are congruent.

B   The sides of figure RSTU are congruent, but the angles are not.

C   The angles of figure RSTU are congruent, but the sides are not.

D   Neither the angles nor the sides of figure RSTU are congruent.

4. Which of the following is **NOT** a right triangle?

A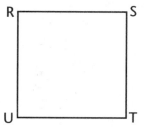

B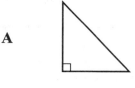

C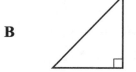

D

Geometry and Spatial Reasoning

Expectation: Identify critical attributes including parallel, perpendicular, and congruent parts of geometric shapes and solids

1. How many edges does a triangular pyramid have?

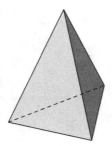

   A 3
   B 4
   C 5
   D 6

2. Figure ABCD is a trapezoid.

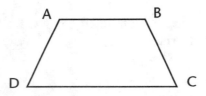

   Which statement is true?

   A $\overline{AB}$ is congruent to $\overline{DC}$.
   B ∠A is congruent to ∠C.
   C $\overline{AD}$ is parallel to $\overline{BC}$.
   D $\overline{AB}$ is parallel to $\overline{DC}$.

3. What is the measure of ∠M?

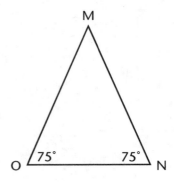

   A 25°
   B 30°
   C 55°
   D 75°

4. How many vertices does a triangular prism have?

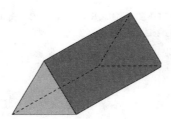

   A 4
   B 5
   C 6
   D 9

Geometry and Spatial Reasoning

Expectation: Identify critical attributes including parallel, perpendicular, and congruent parts of geometric shapes and solids

1. Figure ABC is an isosceles triangle.

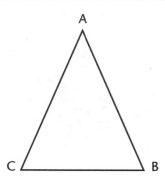

Which statement is **NOT** true?

A $\overline{AB}$ is parallel to $\overline{AC}$.

B $\overline{AB} = \overline{AC}$

C $\angle B = \angle C$

D $\angle A + \angle B + \angle C = 180°$

2. Figure MNOP is a rectangle.

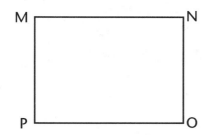

Which statement is true?

A $\overline{MN}$ is congruent to $\overline{NO}$.

B $\overline{MP}$ is congruent to $\overline{OP}$.

C $\overline{MN}$ is parallel to $\overline{PO}$.

D $\overline{NO}$ is parallel to $\overline{MN}$.

3. How many faces does a rectangular prism have?

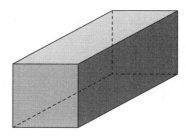

A   3

B   4

C   6

D   8

4. Figure JKLM is a parallelogram.

If $\angle K = 45°$, what is the measure of $\angle M$?

A   10°

B   25°

C   35°

D   45°

1. Which term could **NOT** be used to describe a square?

    A Rectangle
    B Trapezoid
    C Polygon
    D Quadrilateral

2. A polygon with 6 sides is called a—

    A rhombus
    B pentagon
    C hexagon
    D pyramid

3. A cube has 6 faces and—

    A 6 edges
    B 8 edges
    C 10 edges
    D 12 edges

4. Which of the following is **NOT** an attribute of a rectangular prism?

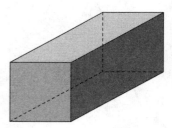

    A 6 faces
    B 8 vertices
    C 10 bases
    D 12 edges

5. Which type of triangle always has at least 2 congruent sides?

    A Isosceles triangle
    B Right triangle
    C Scalene triangle
    D Acute triangle

1. Which of the following is an attribute of a triangular prism?

   A   4 bases
   B   6 faces
   C   9 edges
   D   12 vertices

2. A quadrilateral with only 2 parallel sides is called a—

   A   rhombus
   B   parallelogram
   C   rectangle
   D   trapezoid

3. How many angles does an octagon have?

   A   4
   B   5
   C   6
   D   8

4. Which of the following is an attribute of a scalene triangle?

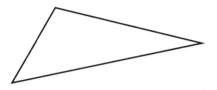

   A   1 right angle
   B   At least 2 congruent sides
   C   No congruent sides
   D   No acute angles

5. Which solid figure has 4 faces and 6 edges?

   A   Triangular pyramid
   B   Rectangular prism
   C   Triangular prism
   D   Cylinder

1. Which of the following is **NOT** an attribute of a rectangle?

    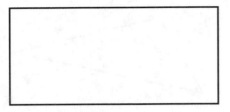

    A   4 right angles
    B   2 sets of parallel sides
    C   2 sets of congruent sides
    D   4 faces

2. The base of a cone is a—

    A   sphere
    B   circle
    C   cylinder
    D   hexagon

3. A pentagon has 5 sides and—

    A   3 angles
    B   4 angles
    C   5 angles
    D   6 angles

4. Which of the following is an attribute of a cube?

    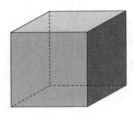

    A   4 faces
    B   6 vertices
    C   10 angles
    D   12 edges

5. Which polygon must have 4 congruent sides?

    A   Rectangle
    B   Rhombus
    C   Parallelogram
    D   Trapezoid

1. Which of the following is an attribute of a square pyramid?

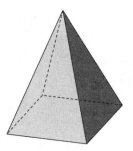

    A 5 faces
    B 5 bases
    C 6 edges
    D 6 vertices

2. The base of a cylinder is a—

    A line
    B sphere
    C square
    D circle

3. All quadrilaterals must have 4 —

    A congruent sides
    B right angles
    C sides
    D acute angles

4. Which of the following is **NOT** an attribute of a triangular pyramid?

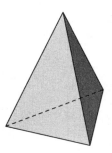

    A 6 edges
    B 4 vertices
    C 4 faces
    D 2 bases

5. A triangle with 3 congruent sides is called—

    A an isosceles triangle
    B a right triangle
    C an equilateral triangle
    D a scalene triangle

Geometry and Spatial Reasoning

*Expectation: Sketch the results of translations,
rotations, and reflections*

1. In which diagram is the unshaded
   figure a rotation of the shaded figure?

2. In which diagram is the unshaded
   figure a reflection of the shaded figure?

A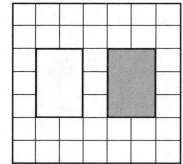

A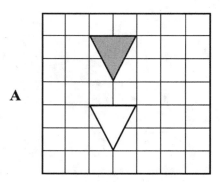

B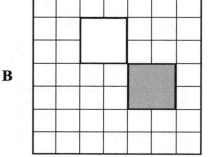

B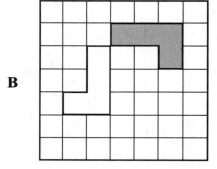

C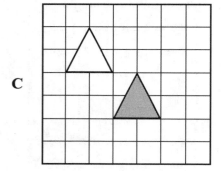

C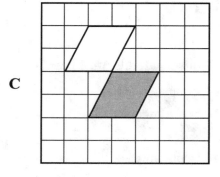

D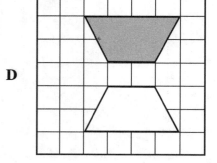

D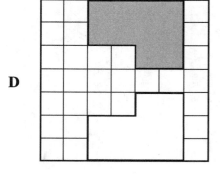

Objective 3
Exercise 10

Geometry and Spatial Reasoning

Expectation: Sketch the results of translations, rotations, and reflections

1. In which diagram is the unshaded figure a translation of the shaded figure?

A
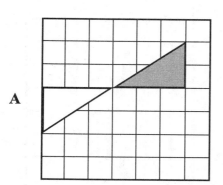

B
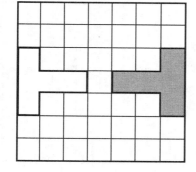

C
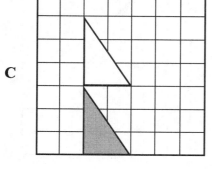

D
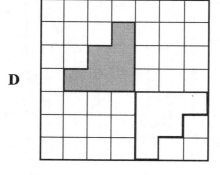

2. In which diagram is the unshaded figure a rotation of the shaded figure?

A
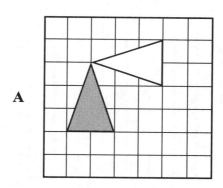

B
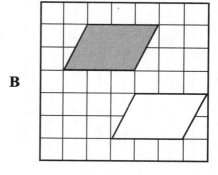

C
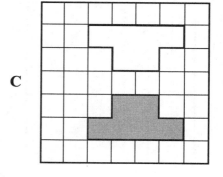

D
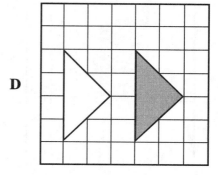

Geometry and Spatial Reasoning

Expectation: Sketch the results of translations, rotations, and reflections

1. In which diagram is the unshaded figure a reflection of the shaded figure?

A
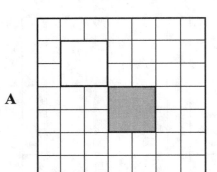

B
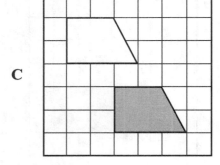

C
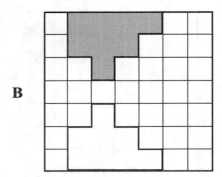

D
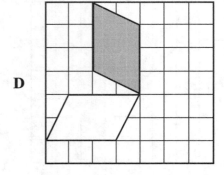

2. In which diagram is the unshaded figure a translation of the shaded figure?

A
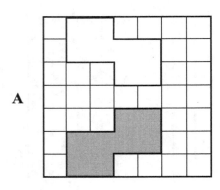

B
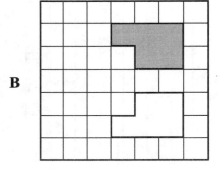

C
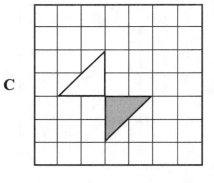

D
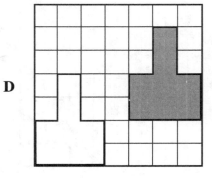

Geometry and Spatial Reasoning

Expectation: Sketch the results of translations, rotations, and reflections

1. In which diagram is the unshaded figure a rotation of the shaded figure?

2. In which diagram is the unshaded figure a reflection of the shaded figure?

A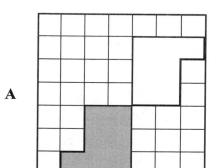

A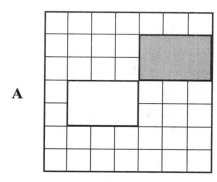

B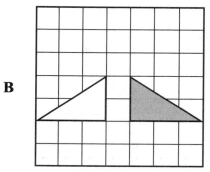

B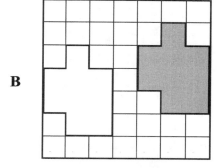

C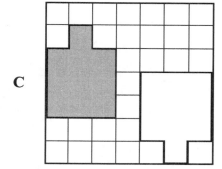

C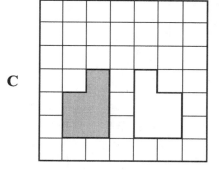

D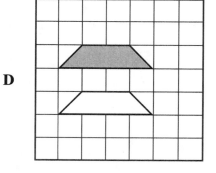

D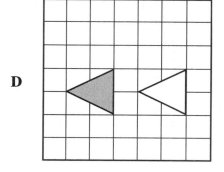

Objective 3
Exercise 13

Geometry and Spatial Reasoning

Expectation: Describe the transformation that generates 1 figure from the other when given 2 congruent figures

1. Which of the following shows an example of a translation?

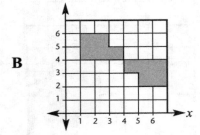

A

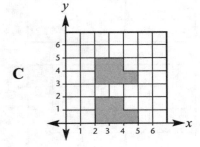

B

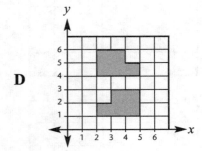

C

D

2. The figures on the graph show an example of a—

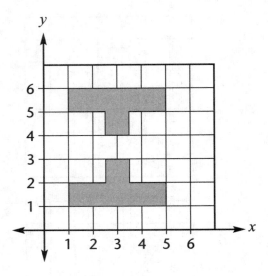

A   rotation

B   translation

C   measurement

D   reflection

Geometry and Spatial Reasoning

Expectation: Describe the transformation that generates 1 figure from the other when given 2 congruent figures

3. Which of the following shows an example of a rotation?

A
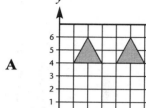

B
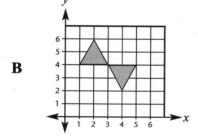

C
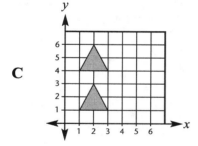

D
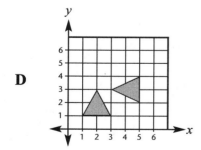

4. The figures on the graph show an example of a—

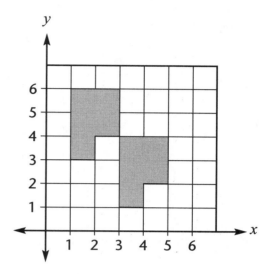

A rotation

B reflection

C translation

D measurement

Geometry and Spatial Reasoning

Expectation: Describe the transformation that generates 1 figure from the other when given 2 congruent figures

1. The figures on the graph show an example of a—

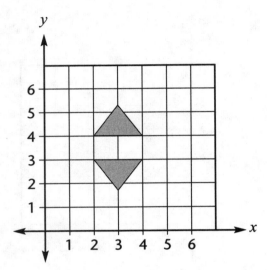

   A rotation
   B reflection
   C translation
   D measurement

2. Which of the following shows an example of a rotation?

A
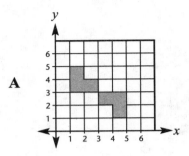

B
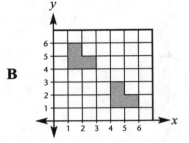

C
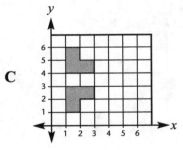

D
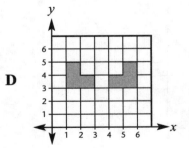

Geometry and Spatial Reasoning

Expectation: Describe the transformation that generates 1 figure from the other when given 2 congruent figures

3. Which of the following shows an example of a reflection?

A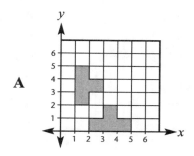

B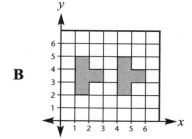

C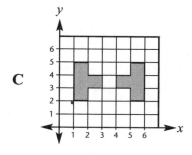

D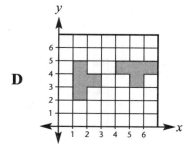

4. The figures on the graph show an example of a—

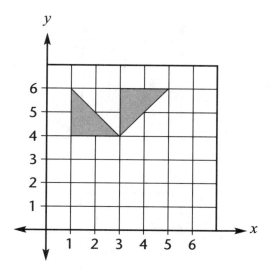

A reflection

B rotation

C translation

D measurement

Geometry and Spatial Reasoning

1. Which of the following does **NOT** show an example of a translation?

A
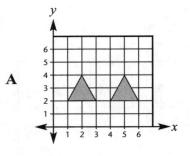

B
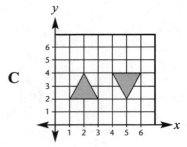

C
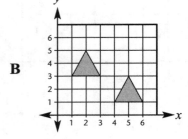

D
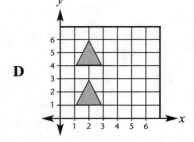

2. Which of the following does **NOT** show an example of a reflection?

A
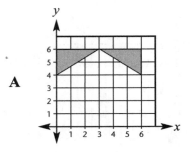

B
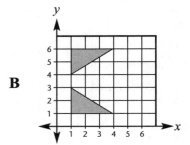

C
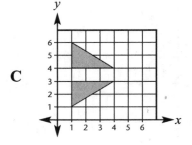

D
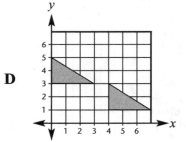

Geometry and Spatial Reasoning

Expectation: Describe the transformation that generates 1 figure from the other when given 2 congruent figures

3. The figures on the graph show an example of a—

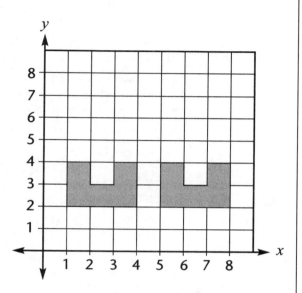

A rotation
B reflection
C property
D translation

4. Which of the following shows an example of a rotation?

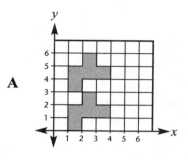

A

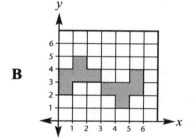

B

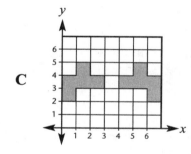

C

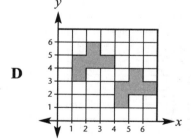

D

Geometry and Spatial Reasoning

Expectation: Locate and name points on a coordinate grid using ordered pairs of whole numbers

1. Which point on the graph best identifies the ordered pair (2, 4)?

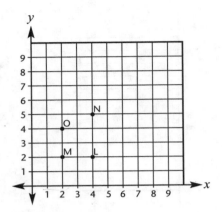

   A L

   B M

   C N

   D O

2. Which point on the graph best identifies the ordered pair (3, 7)?

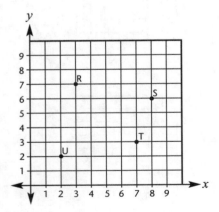

   A R

   B S

   C T

   D U

3. Point P best represents which ordered pair?

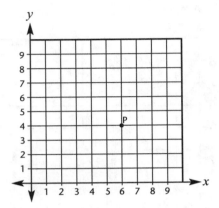

   A (4, 6)

   B (5, 3)

   C (6, 4)

   D (6, 6)

4. Point R best represents which ordered pair?

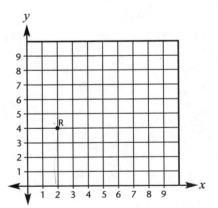

   A (5, 2)

   B (5, 3)

   C (2, 6)

   D (2, 4)

Geometry and Spatial Reasoning

Expectation: Locate and name points on a coordinate grid using ordered pairs of whole numbers

1. Which letter on the graph best identifies the ordered pair (5, 7)?

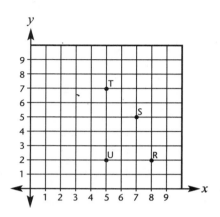

  A   R

  B   S

  C   T

  D   U

3. Point T best represents which ordered pair?

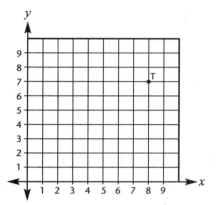

  A   (7, 8)

  B   (8, 7)

  C   (8, 6)

  D   (9, 5)

2. Point G best represents which ordered pair?

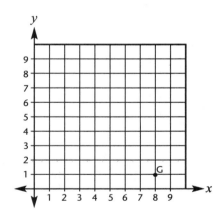

  A   (1, 8)

  B   (2, 8)

  C   (7, 1)

  D   (8, 1)

4. Which point best represents the ordered pair (4, 5)?

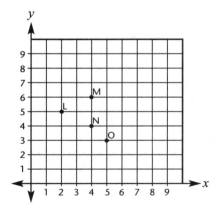

  A   O

  B   N

  C   M

  D   L

1. Which ordered pair is inside the triangle?

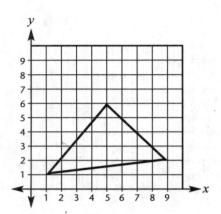

  A (2, 3)

  B (3, 2)

  C (4, 1)

  D (6, 6)

2. Which ordered pair is **NOT** inside the rectangle?

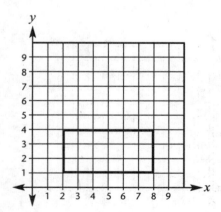

  A (3, 2)

  B (3, 5)

  C (4, 3)

  D (5, 3)

3. Point M best represents which ordered pair?

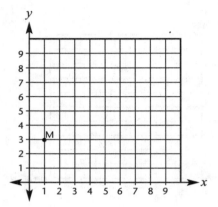

  A (4, 2)

  B (3, 1)

  C (2, 1)

  D (1, 3)

4. Which point best represents the ordered pair (9, 4)?

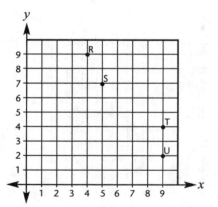

  A R

  B S

  C T

  D U

1. Which ordered pair is inside the triangle?

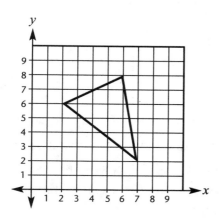

  A (4, 4)
  B (5, 3)
  C (6, 7)
  D (7, 6)

2. Which ordered pair is **NOT** inside the circle?

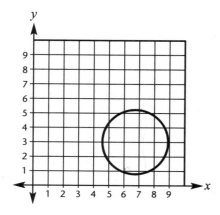

  A (7, 5)
  B (6, 1)
  C (5, 3)
  D (1, 6)

3. Which ordered pair best represents point J?

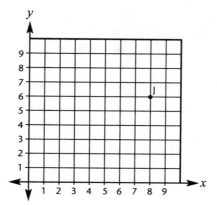

  A (6, 8)
  B (7, 5)
  C (7, 7)
  D (8, 6)

4. Which ordered pair best represents point K?

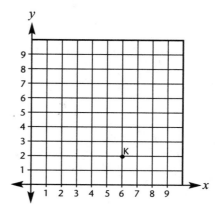

  A (6, 2)
  B (6, 1)
  C (5, 4)
  D (2, 6)

Objective 4

Measurement

A. Measure volume using models of cubic units

B. Measure to solve problems involving length (including perimeter), weight, capacity, time, temperature, and area

C. Describe numerical relationships between units of measure within the same measurement system, such as an inch is $\frac{1}{12}$ of a foot

Measurement

Expectation: Measure volume using models of cubic units

1. A cube made of 1-inch cubes is shown below.

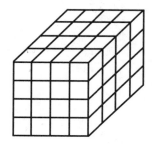

   What is the volume of this cube?

   A 12 in³

   B 32 in³

   C 48 in³

   D 64 in³

2. A rectangular prism made of 1-foot cubes is shown below.

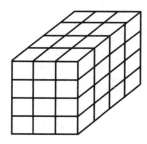

   What is the volume of this rectangular prism?

   A 33 ft³

   B 36 ft³

   C 48 ft³

   D 64 ft³

3. Which model shows a prism with a volume of 18 cubic units?

   A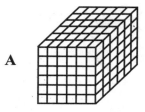

   B

   C

   D

4. A rectangular prism made of 1-centimeter cubes is shown below.

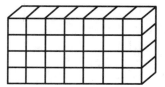

   What is the volume of this rectangular prism?

   A 12 cm³

   B 21 cm³

   C 28 cm³

   D 39 cm³

1. A cube made of 1-inch cubes is
   shown below.

   What is the volume of this cube?

   A 6 in³
   B 8 in³
   C 12 in³
   D 16 in³

2. A rectangular prism made of
   1-centimeter cubes is shown below.

   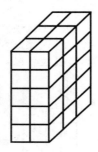

   What is the volume of this rectangular
   prism?

   A 15 cm³
   B 25 cm³
   C 30 cm³
   D 46 cm³

3. Which model shows a prism with a
   volume of 125 cubic units?

   A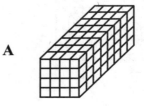

   B

   C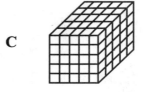

   D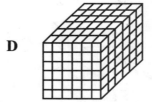

4. A rectangular prism is made of
   1-centimeter cubes. The volume of the
   rectangular prism is 60 cubic
   centimeters. Which set of dimensions
   could describe the rectangular prism?

   A 2 cm × 3 cm × 4 cm
   B 3 cm × 3 cm × 5 cm
   C 3 cm × 4 cm × 5 cm
   D 30 cm × 30 cm

Measurement

Expectation: Measure volume using models of cubic units

1. A rectangular prism made of 1-foot cubes is shown below.

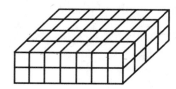

What is the volume of this rectangular prism?

A 13 ft³

B 28 ft³

C 50 ft³

D 56 ft³

2. Which model shows a prism with a volume of 20 cubic units?

A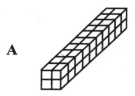

B

C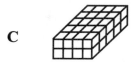

D

3. A rectangular prism made of 1-foot cubes is shown below.

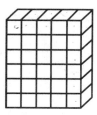

What is the volume of this rectangular prism?

A 30 ft³

B 31 ft³

C 41 ft³

D 150 ft³

4. Benjamin bought a set of blocks for his little brother. He notices that each block is a cube, and all of the blocks fit exactly in the rectangular package.

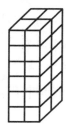

What is the volume of the rectangular package?

A 28 cubic units

B 24 cubic units

C 12 cubic units

D 10 cubic units

Measurement

Expectation: Measure to solve problems involving length (including perimeter), weight, capacity, time, temperature, and area

1. What is the **perimeter** of this polygon?

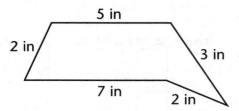

   A 10 in
   B 14 in
   C 17 in
   D 19 in

2. What is the **volume** of the cube in the diagram?

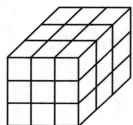

   A 9 cubic units
   B 12 cubic units
   C 18 cubic units
   D 27 cubic units

3. Dustin set his alarm clock for 5:30 a.m., but woke up 45 minutes before the alarm rang. At what time did Dustin wake up?

   A 6:15 a.m.
   B 5:00 a.m.
   C 4:50 a.m.
   D 4:45 a.m.

4. Kai is 5 feet 4 inches tall. His father is 5 feet 11 inches tall. How much taller than Kai is his father?

   A 15 in
   B 10 in
   C 7 in
   D 4 in

5. The diagram shows a rectangular bedspread. Each square equals 1 square foot.

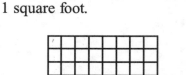

   What is the **area** of the bedspread?

   A 28 ft²
   B 40 ft²
   C 48 ft²
   D 56 ft²

6. At a basketball camp, Carlos dribbled the ball 100 feet 6 inches without stopping. Donna dribbled the ball 110 feet 4 inches without stopping. How much farther would Carlos need to dribble to equal the distance that Donna dribbled?

   A 110 feet 2 inches
   B 9 feet 6 inches
   C 10 feet 2 inches
   D 9 feet 10 inches

Measurement

Expectation: Measure to solve problems involving length (including perimeter), weight, capacity, time, temperature, and area

1. Mrs. Ramos bought 4 pounds 3 ounces of bananas, 2 pounds 8 ounces of apples, and 1 pound 4 ounces of grapes. What was the combined weight of the fruit Mrs. Ramos bought?

   A 7 lb 15 oz

   B 8 lb 5 oz

   C 8 lb 10 oz

   D 22 lb

2. Kate is making a cake that must bake at 350°F for 40 minutes. The oven in her kitchen reads 275°F. How much hotter does the oven need to be?

   A 425°F

   B 125°F

   C 75°F

   D 40°F

3. Mrs. Douglas has a new wall-to-wall carpet in her classroom. If her rectangular classroom measures 20 feet by 24 feet, what is the area covered by carpet?

   A 480 ft²

   B 360 ft²

   C 200 ft²

   D 88 ft²

4. Mr. Brewer drives to and from work each day. He travels 40 minutes each way. How much time does he spend driving to and from work each day?

   A 40 min

   B 1 hr 10 min

   C 1 hr 20 min

   D 1 hr 40 min

5. What is the **volume** of a rectangular prism that is 3 feet tall, 4 feet wide, and 3 feet long?

   A 38 ft³

   B 36 ft³

   C 15 ft³

   D 10 ft³

Objective 4
Exercise 6

Measurement

Expectation: Measure to solve problems involving length (including perimeter), weight, capacity, time, temperature, and area

1. What is the **perimeter** of the shaded area?

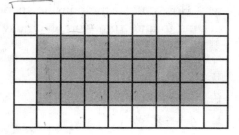

    A 16 units

    B 21 units

    C 24 units

    D 28 units

2. A rectangular prism is 4 centimeters tall, 4 centimeters wide, and 3 centimeters long. What is the **volume** of the rectangular prism?

    A 24 cm³

    B 28 cm³

    C 36 cm³

    D 48 cm³

3. On Monday, Nancy studied for 1 hour and 10 minutes. On Tuesday, she studied for 55 minutes. On Wednesday, she studied for 1 hour and 15 minutes. How long did Nancy study during the 3-day period?

    A 3 hr 20 min

    B 3 hr 30 min

    C 4 hr 10 min

    D 4 hr 40 min

4. Mason built a rock border around the flower bed shown in the diagram. How long was the entire rock border?

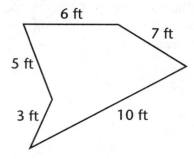

    A 26 ft

    B 28 ft

    C 30 ft

    D 31 ft

5. Greg has 2 puppies named Marco and Burt. Burt weighs 35 pounds 10 ounces. Marco weighs 16 pounds 14 ounces. How much more does Burt weigh than Marco?

    A 18 lb

    B 18 lb 4 oz

    C 18 lb 12 oz

    D 19 lb 10 oz

6. Molly arrived at the gym at 8:25. She exercised for 1 hour and 40 minutes and then went home. What time did Molly leave the gym?

    A 9:30

    B 9:45

    C 10:00

    D 10:05

Measurement

Expectation: Measure to solve problems involving length (including perimeter), weight, capacity, time, temperature, and area

1. Mel had 1.1 meters of wire. He needed 200 centimeters of wire for one project and 150 centimeters for another project. How much more wire did Mel need to do both projects?

   A   4.6 m

   B   3.5 m

   C   2.4 m

   D   1.5 m

2. When Jason began jogging, it was 70°F. Halfway through his jog, the temperature had gone up 3°F. At the end of his jog, the temperature had gone up 5°F more. What was the temperature at the end of his jog?

   A   78°F

   B   75°F

   C   72°F

   D   62°F

3. Ahn's puppy weighed 3.2 kilograms in May. It gained 800 grams in June and 1.2 kilograms in July. How much did the puppy weigh then?

   A   4.4 kg

   B   5.2 kg

   C   5.8 kg

   D   6.1 kg

4. Broad Street is perpendicular to Main Street.

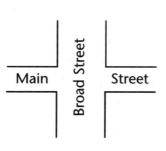

   How many right angles are formed at the intersection of the 2 streets?

   A   1

   B   2

   C   3

   D   4

5. Jared walked 1 lap around the neighborhood's 10.8-kilometer track each day.

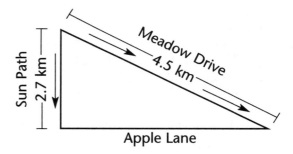

   How far did Jared walk along Apple Lane?

   A   6.0 km

   B   3.6 km

   C   3.0 km

   D   2.2 km

Measurement

Expectation: Measure to solve problems involving length (including perimeter), weight, capacity, time, temperature, and area

1. In the morning, Devonia studied for her math test from 10:15 a.m. until 11:00 a.m. In the afternoon, she studied from 2:30 p.m. until 3:15 p.m. What is the total amount of time Devonia studied for her math test?

    A 2 hr 30 min

    B 2 hr 15 min

    C 1 hr 45 min

    D 1 hr 30 min

2. Shannon is making cookies and must preheat the oven to 350°F. The oven thermometer shows 275°F. How much hotter must the oven be before Shannon can bake the cookies?

    A 25°F

    B 50°F

    C 75°F

    D 100°F

3. A jug holds 1 quart of milk. Matt uses 1 pint of the milk to make pancakes. Then, Alex uses 1 cup of the milk on his cereal. How much milk is left in the jug?

    A 1 c

    B 1 qt

    C 2 c

    D 1 pt

4. Mrs. Perez scheduled 2 hours for oral book reports on Friday afternoon. Roland's report took 10 minutes, Jerome's report took 15 minutes, and Carla's report took 10 minutes. How much time was left for reports by other students?

    A 1 hr 25 min

    B 1 hr 35 min

    C 1 hr 40 min

    D 1 hr 45 min

5. A pitcher holds 2 liters of juice. Miranda has 4 juice glasses that can each hold 300 milliliters. If Miranda fills each glass with juice, how much juice will be left in the pitcher?

    A 1,700 mL

    B 1,000 mL

    C 800 mL

    D 500 mL

Measurement

Expectation: Measure to solve problems involving length (including perimeter), weight, capacity, time, temperature, and area

1. Mrs. Morgan wants to sew beaded trim to the edges of 2 tablecloths. One tablecloth is 5 feet long and 4 feet wide. The other is 6 feet long and 4 feet wide. What is the total amount of beaded trim Mrs. Morgan will use on the tablecloths?

    A   30 ft
    B   38 ft
    C   44 ft
    D   54 ft

2. Mr. Clarkson ordered wall-to-wall carpeting for 2 classrooms. Each classroom is 20 feet long and 20 feet wide. How much carpeting did Mr. Clarkson order?

    A   800 ft²
    B   600 ft²
    C   400 ft²
    D   80 ft²

3. For a science experiment, water must be heated to 100°C. If Tucker begins with water that is 72°C, by how many degrees must he heat it for the experiment?

    A   172°C
    B   38°C
    C   32°C
    D   28°C

4. At 9:00 a.m., the outside temperature was 74°F. If the temperature went up 3°F every hour, what was the temperature at 1:00 p.m.?

    A   86°F
    B   83°F
    C   80°F
    D   77°F

5. On Monday, a swimming pool had 5 feet 6 inches of water. If the water level dropped 2 inches every day after Monday, what was the water level on the following Saturday morning?

    A   5 ft 4 in
    B   5 ft
    C   4 ft 8 in
    D   4 ft 6 in

Objective 4
Exercise 10

Measurement

Expectation: Describe numerical relationships between units of measure within the same measurement system, such as an inch is $\frac{1}{12}$ of a foot

1. Tanya bought a water bowl for her cat. The bowl holds 500 milliliters of water. What fraction of a liter is 500 milliliters?

   A $\frac{3}{4}$

   B $\frac{2}{3}$

   C $\frac{1}{2}$

   D $\frac{1}{3}$

2. Which of the following is true?

   A 80 cm > 0.9 m

   B 800 cm = 0.8 m

   C 800 cm < 800 mm

   D 800 mm = 0.8 m

3. Which unit of measure is $\frac{1}{1000}$ of a kilometer?

   A 1 meter

   B 1 decimeter

   C 1 centimeter

   D 1 millimeter

4. Which unit of measure is $\frac{1}{4}$ of a gallon?

   A 1 ounce

   B 1 cup

   C 1 pint

   D 1 quart

5. What fraction of 1 yard is 1 foot?

   A $\frac{1}{2}$

   B $\frac{1}{3}$

   C $\frac{1}{4}$

   D $\frac{1}{12}$

6. Which of the following is true?

   A 10 in > 1 ft

   B 24 in < 1 ft

   C 24 in < 1 yd

   D 36 in > 1 yd

Measurement

Expectation: Describe numerical relationships between units of measure within the same measurement system, such as an inch is $\frac{1}{12}$ of a foot

1. Which of the following is $\frac{1}{3}$ of an hour?

   A   10 min

   B   15 min

   C   20 min

   D   30 min

2. Which of the following is true?

   A   24 oz = 1 lb 8 oz

   B   24 oz = 2 lb

   C   20 oz < 1 lb

   D   1 lb 8 oz > 28 oz

3. The chart shows the height of 4 trees on Mr. Jansen's property.

Tree	Height
Maple	235 cm
Apple	1.9 m
Oak	1.85 m
Pine	300 cm

   Which tree is the tallest?

   A   Maple

   B   Apple

   C   Oak

   D   Pine

4. Which unit of measure is $\frac{1}{10}$ of a meter?

   A   1 millimeter

   B   1 centimeter

   C   1 decimeter

   D   1 kilometer

5. Which unit of measure is $\frac{1}{8}$ of a cup?

   A   1 ounce

   B   1 pint

   C   1 quart

   D   1 gallon

6. Which of the following is true?

   A   1.2 kg = 12,000 g

   B   1.2 kg < 800 g

   C   1.2 kg > 1,500 g

   D   1.2 kg = 1,200 g

Objective 4
Exercise 12

Measurement

Expectation: Describe numerical relationships between units of measure within the same measurement system, such as an inch is $\frac{1}{12}$ of a foot

1. Which of the following is $\frac{1}{10}$ of an hour?

   A 12 min
   B 10 min
   C 8 min
   D 6 min

2. Which of the following is true?

   A 1.6 L = 1,600 mL
   B 1.6 L < 1,400 mL
   C 1,200 mL < 1 L
   D 1,200 mL > 1.5 L

3. Which unit of measure is $\frac{1}{2}$ of a quart?

   A 1 gallon
   B 1 pint
   C 1 cup
   D 1 ounce

4. Which of the following is $\frac{1}{2}$ of 5 hours?

   A 50 min
   B 150 min
   C 250 min
   D 300 min

5. Jerry spent $\frac{1}{4}$ of a day outside playing in the water. How long did Jerry play in the water?

   A 6 hr
   B 5 hr
   C 4 hr
   D 3 hr

6. A jug held 12 pints of milk. Tina drank $\frac{1}{3}$ of the milk. How much milk did Tina drink?

   A 1 gal
   B 2 qt
   C 1 qt
   D 1 pt

**Objective 4
Exercise 13**

Measurement

Expectation: Describe numerical relationships between units of measure within the same measurement system, such as an inch is $\frac{1}{12}$ of a foot

1. Which of the following is $\frac{1}{3}$ of a day?

   A 4 hr
   B 6 hr
   C 8 hr
   D 10 hr

2. Which of the following is true?

   A 1,400 g > 10 kg
   B 1,000 g > 1.2 kg
   C 1,900 g = 19 kg
   D 1,400 g = 1.4 kg

3. Which unit of measure is $\frac{1}{10}$ of a centimeter?

   A 1 millimeter
   B 1 decimeter
   C 1 kilometer
   D 1 meter

4. Mari was in the library for 3 hours. She spent $\frac{1}{3}$ of the time studying for her science test. How long did Mari study science?

   A 90 min
   B 60 min
   C 45 min
   D 30 min

5. Which unit of measure is $\frac{1}{2}$ of a pint?

   A 1 ounce
   B 1 cup
   C 1 quart
   D 1 gallon

6. Philip used 4 ounces of nuts to make fudge. What fraction of a pound is 4 ounces?

   A $\frac{3}{4}$
   B $\frac{2}{3}$
   C $\frac{1}{2}$
   D $\frac{1}{4}$

Objective 5

Probability and Statistics

A. Use fractions to describe the results of
   an experiment

B. Use experimental results to make predictions

C. Use tables of related number pairs to make
   line graphs

D. Describe characteristics of data presented in tables
   and graphs, including the shape and spread of the
   data and the middle number

E. Graph a given set of data using an appropriate
   graphical representation, such as a picture or a line

1. A bag contains 3 red counting chips
   and 4 yellow counting chips. If you pull
   a chip from the bag without looking,
   what is the probability of choosing a
   yellow chip?

   A $\frac{1}{4}$

   B $\frac{3}{7}$

   C $\frac{3}{4}$

   D $\frac{4}{7}$

2. A bag of candy has 6 candies in it.
   There are 2 cherry candies, 1 lime
   candy, 2 berry candies, and 1 orange
   candy. What is the probability of
   choosing a cherry candy if you choose
   it without looking in the bag?

   A $\frac{1}{6}$

   B $\frac{1}{3}$

   C $\frac{1}{2}$

   D $\frac{2}{3}$

3. Of 8 tickets in a jar, 3 have winning
   numbers. If you select a ticket from
   the jar without looking, what is
   the probability of selecting a
   winning ticket?

   A $\frac{1}{5}$

   B $\frac{1}{3}$

   C $\frac{3}{8}$

   D $\frac{5}{8}$

4. You have 7 T-shirts in your drawer.
   Only 2 of them are red. If you choose
   a shirt from the drawer without
   looking, what is the probability of
   choosing a shirt that is **NOT** red?

   A $\frac{5}{7}$

   B $\frac{1}{2}$

   C $\frac{2}{7}$

   D $\frac{1}{7}$

1. You have several new pencils in a drawer: 1 red, 2 blue, 2 green, and 1 yellow. If you take 1 pencil from the drawer without looking, what is the probability that it will be red?

   A $\frac{1}{6}$

   B $\frac{1}{3}$

   C $\frac{1}{2}$

   D $\frac{5}{6}$

2. Mrs. Frank has jelly beans in a small jar. There are 5 cherry, 3 lime, 1 orange, and 1 licorice. If she takes 1 jelly bean from the jar without looking, what is the probability that it will be lime?

   A $\frac{1}{2}$

   B $\frac{3}{7}$

   C $\frac{1}{3}$

   D $\frac{3}{10}$

3. A jar had 5 red marbles and 2 white marbles. Adam took 1 marble from the jar without looking and then placed it back in the jar. Then, Sandra chose 1 marble from the jar without looking. What is the probability of Sandra choosing a white marble?

   A $\frac{5}{7}$

   B $\frac{1}{3}$

   C $\frac{2}{7}$

   D $\frac{1}{7}$

4. The spinner is divided into 4 equal sections. What is the probability of the arrow landing on blue when you spin?

   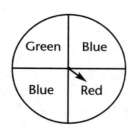

   A $\frac{1}{4}$

   B $\frac{1}{3}$

   C $\frac{1}{2}$

   D $\frac{2}{3}$

1. A box contains tickets of different colors. The chart shows how many tickets there are of each color.

Color	Number
Red	3
Blue	4
Green	1
Orange	2

If you reach into the box without looking and take a ticket, what is the probability of choosing a green ticket?

A $\frac{1}{10}$

B $\frac{1}{8}$

C $\frac{3}{10}$

D $\frac{9}{10}$

2. Mrs. Lee is a teller in a bank. She has 8 keys on a key ring. All the keys look the same, but only 4 will open teller drawers. What is the probability that the first key she tries will **NOT** be a key for a teller drawer?

A $\frac{1}{8}$

B $\frac{1}{3}$

C $\frac{1}{2}$

D $\frac{2}{3}$

3. The spinner is divided into 6 equal sections. What is the probability of the arrow landing on the square when you spin?

A $\frac{1}{6}$

B $\frac{1}{5}$

C $\frac{1}{3}$

D $\frac{5}{6}$

4. Carmen has 3 cherry lollipops, 1 lemon lollipop, and 1 grape lollipop in her purse. If she reaches in her purse without looking and takes a lollipop, what is the probability that it will be grape?

A $\frac{3}{5}$

B $\frac{1}{3}$

C $\frac{1}{4}$

D $\frac{1}{5}$

1. A teacher placed 7 tokens in a bag. The tokens were the same, except 1 had the word "winner" on it. If a student takes a token from the bag without looking, what is the probability that the student will **NOT** pick the "winner" token?

    A $\frac{6}{7}$

    B $\frac{1}{6}$

    C $\frac{1}{7}$

    D $\frac{1}{8}$

2. Paul has a drawer of "odd" socks that have no matches. There are 5 green socks, 1 red sock, 1 gray sock, 1 black sock, and 2 blue socks. If Paul takes a sock from the drawer without looking, what is the probability that it will be either green or blue?

    A $\frac{3}{10}$

    B $\frac{2}{5}$

    C $\frac{1}{2}$

    D $\frac{7}{10}$

3. The spinner is divided into 8 equal sections. What is the probability of the arrow landing on R or S when you spin?

    A $\frac{2}{3}$

    B $\frac{5}{8}$

    C $\frac{3}{8}$

    D $\frac{1}{4}$

4. The spinner is divided into 4 equal sections. What is the probability of the arrow landing on an even number when you spin?

    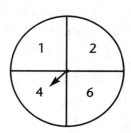

    A $\frac{3}{4}$

    B $\frac{1}{2}$

    C $\frac{1}{3}$

    D $\frac{1}{4}$

1. In a total of 25 spins, which color will the arrow probably point to the **greatest** number of times?

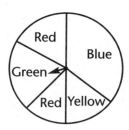

   A Yellow
   B Red
   C Green
   D Blue

2. A box contains 5 balls. They are the same size and same shape, but the patterns vary.

   Which is a possible outcome if 3 balls are selected from the box at the same time?

   A
   B
   C
   D

3. A spinner is divided into 5 equal sections. Each section is marked with a circle, a square, or a triangle. The spinner is spun 20 times. The chart shows the results.

   Spinner Results

Shape	Number of Spins
○	卌
□	|||
△	卌 卌 ||

   Based on the results shown in the chart, which is the best prediction of the number of sections marked with a circle, square, or triangle?

   A 3 circles, 1 square, 1 triangle
   B 2 circles, 2 squares, 1 triangle
   C 1 circle, 1 square, 3 triangles
   D 1 circle, 2 squares, 2 triangles

4. Isabel spun the spinner 30 times. Based on the spinner's layout, which is the best prediction of the results of Isabel's spins?

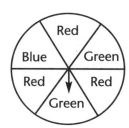

   A 10 blue, 15 green, 5 red
   B 5 blue, 20 green, 5 red
   C 5 blue, 15 green, 10 red
   D 5 blue, 10 green, 15 red

1. A prize box contains 20 tickets marked with 1 of 2 prizes: a candy bar or stickers. Each of 25 students selected a ticket without looking, put it back in the box, and recorded the prize on the chart.

   Ticket Selection

Prize	Number of Selections
Candy Bar	~~卌~~ ~~卌~~ |||
Stickers	~~卌~~ ~~卌~~ ||

   Based on the results shown in the chart, which is the best prediction for the number of each type of ticket in the box?

   A   15 candy bars and 5 stickers

   B   12 candy bars and 8 stickers

   C   10 candy bars and 10 stickers

   D   8 candy bars and 12 stickers

2. In a total of 10 spins, which shape will the spinner probably point to the **fewest** number of times?

   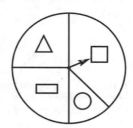

   A   △

   B   ▭

   C   □

   D   ○

3. A bag contains 5 balls. The balls are the same size and same shape, but they vary in color.

   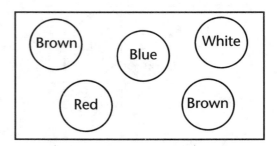

   Which outcome is **NOT** possible if 3 balls are selected from the box at the same time?

   A   Brown, blue, brown

   B   White, red, blue

   C   Brown, red, blue

   D   White, red, white

4. In a total of 12 spins, which number will the arrow probably point to the **greatest** number of times?

   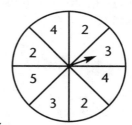

   A   5

   B   4

   C   3

   D   2

Probability and Statistics

Expectation: Use experimental results to make predictions

1. Without looking, Delaney selected a chip from the box. Based on the chips you see in the picture, which is the best prediction of the type of chip Delaney selected?

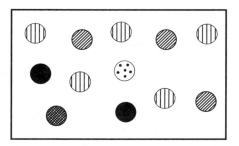

A

B

C

D

2. In a total of 15 spins, which name will the arrow probably point to the **greatest** number of times?

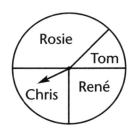

A   Chris

B   René

C   Rosie

D   Tom

3. A box holds 6 new pencils. The pencils are the same size and shape, but they vary in color.

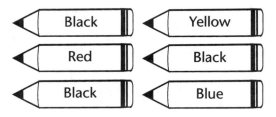

Which is a possible outcome if 3 pencils are selected from the box at the same time?

A   Black, red, red

B   Yellow, yellow, yellow

C   Black, black, black

D   Blue, red, blue

4. A box of straws contains 12 straws. Some of the straws are striped, and some are plain. Each of 20 students took a straw from the box without looking, put the straw back in the box, and recorded the pattern on the chart.

Pattern	Number
Striped	⳽ I
Plain	⳽ ⳽ IIII

Based on the results shown in the chart, which is the best prediction of the number of each type of straw in the box?

A   1 striped straw and 11 plain straws

B   3 striped straws and 9 plain straws

C   6 striped straws and 6 plain straws

D   9 striped straws and 3 plain straws

1. A bowl contains 15 chips that are the same size and same shape but marked with different letters.

   If you select a chip from the bowl without looking, which letter will you **most likely** select?

   A X
   B T
   C S
   D R

2. A box contains 12 marbles. The marbles are different colors. Each of 15 children selected a marble without looking, put the marble back, and recorded the results on the chart.

   Marble Selection

Color	Number of Times
Black	|||
White	||||
Blue	~~||||~~ |||

   Based on the results shown in the chart, which is the best prediction of the number of black, white, and blue marbles in the box?

   A 3 black, 3 white, 6 blue
   B 4 black, 6 white, 2 blue
   C 5 black, 5 white, 2 blue
   D 1 black, 5 white, 6 blue

3. Jacob spun the spinner 20 times. Based on the spinner's layout, which is the best prediction of the results of Jacob's spins?

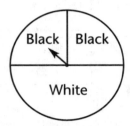

   A 5 black and 15 white
   B 6 black and 14 white
   C 10 black and 10 white
   D 15 black and 5 white

4. Grace spun the spinner 20 times. She landed on a certain symbol only once. Which symbol would that **most likely** be?

   A ♦
   B ♥
   C ♣
   D ★

Probability and Statistics

Expectation: Use tables of related number pairs to make line graphs

1. The chart shows the temperature during 1 day.

Time of Day	Temperature	Time of Day	Temperature
6 a.m.	40°F	10 a.m.	52°F
7 a.m.	44°F	11 a.m.	52°F
8 a.m.	48°F	12 p.m.	52°F
9 a.m.	50°F	1 p.m.	48°F

Which graph correctly represents the data in the chart?

A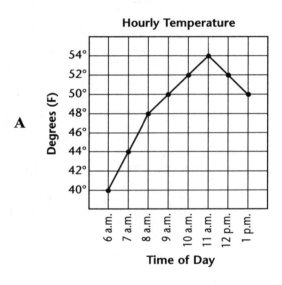

C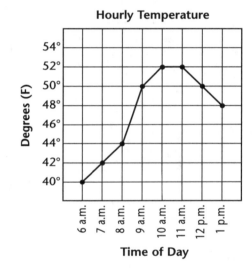

B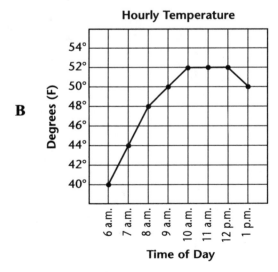

D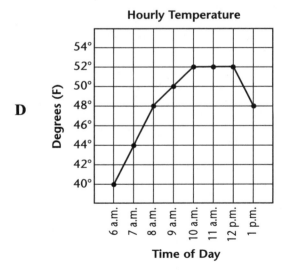

Probability and Statistics

Expectation: Use tables of related number pairs to make line graphs

2. On which coordinate plane does the number line pass through ordered pairs
    (1, 1) and (3, 3)?

A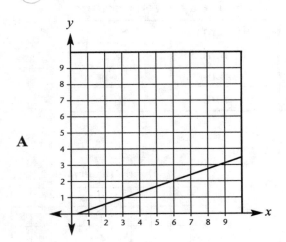

C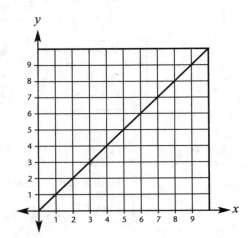

B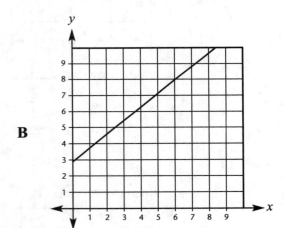

D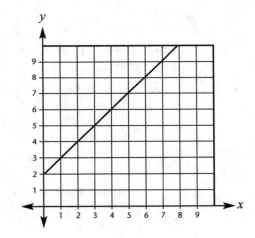

Probability and Statistics

Expectation: Use tables of related number pairs to make line graphs

1. On which coordinate plane does the number line pass through ordered pairs (3, 4) and (4, 5)?

A

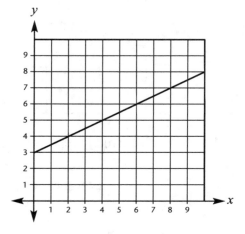

B

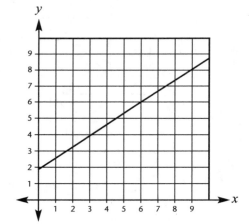

C

D

2. The chart shows the amount of rain collected in rain gauges at different elevations during a 24-hour period.

Elevation	Rainfall	Elevation	Rainfall
250 ft	1.5 in	1,250 ft	2.5 in
500 ft	1.0 in	1,500 ft	2.5 in
750 ft	1.5 in	1,750 ft	3.0 in
1,000 ft	2.0 in	2,000 ft	3.5 in

Which graph correctly represents the data in the chart?

A
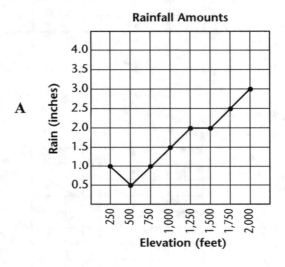

C
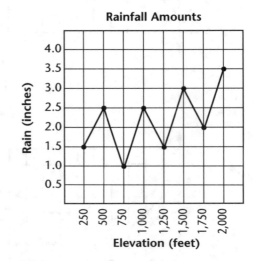

B
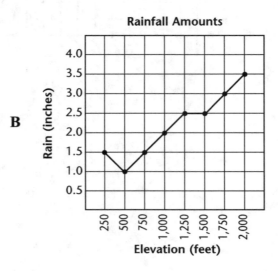

D
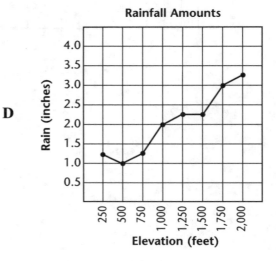

Probability and Statistics

Expectation: Use tables of related number pairs to make line graphs

1. On which coordinate plane does the number line pass through ordered pairs (5, 4) and (7, 5)?

A

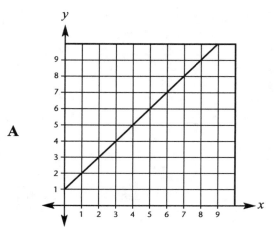

C

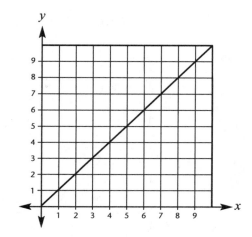

B

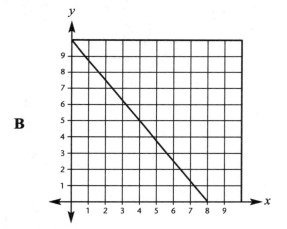

D

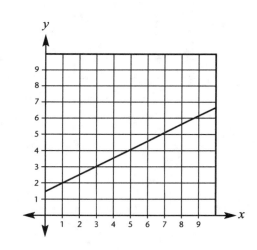

2. The chart shows how many students went to the nurse's office during each period of a school day.

Period	Student	Period	Student
1	12	5	12
2	6	6	13
3	8	7	15
4	10	8	7

Which graph correctly represents the data in the chart?

A
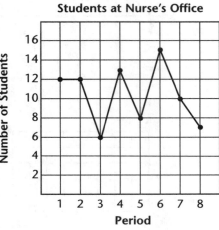

C
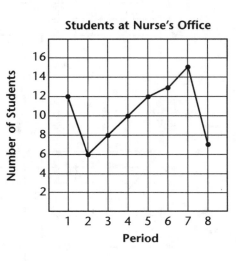

B
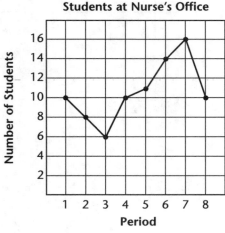

D
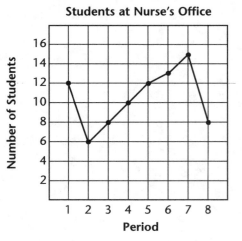

Probability and Statistics

Expectation: Describe characteristics of data presented in tables and graphs, including the shape and spread of the data and the middle number

The graph shows the number of books borrowed from the school library by several classes during March. Use the graph to answer questions 1–3.

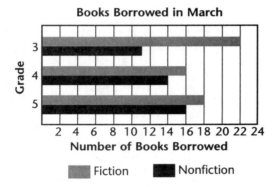

1. How many nonfiction books did the fourth-grade class borrow from the school library?

   A 7

   B 12

   C 14

   D 16

2. What was the **range** of nonfiction books borrowed by the different classes?

   A 10

   B 8

   C 6

   D 5

3. How many more fiction books did the third-grade class borrow than the fifth-grade class?

   A 4

   B 6

   C 30

   D 40

The graph shows the number of student absences at school during a 10-day period. Use the graph to answer questions 4–6.

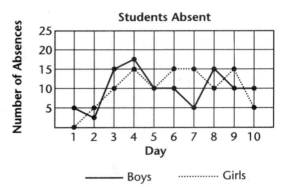

4. How many girls were absent on day 5?

   A 15

   B 10

   C 5

   D 3

5. On which day were the greatest number of students absent?

   A Day 3

   B Day 4

   C Day 7

   D Day 8

6. On which day was there the greatest difference in the number of girls and number of boys who were absent?

   A Day 1

   B Day 4

   C Day 6

   D Day 7

Probability and Statistics

Expectation: Describe characteristics of data presented in tables and graphs, including the shape and spread of the data and the middle number

The graph shows the average high and low temperatures for 5 Texas cities in January. Use the graph to answer questions 1 and 2.

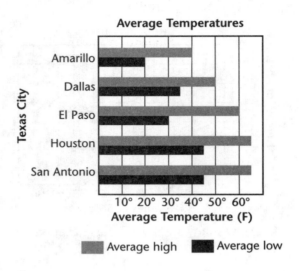

The graph shows the number of recorded tornadoes in Texas during 1987. Use the graph to answer questions 3 and 4.

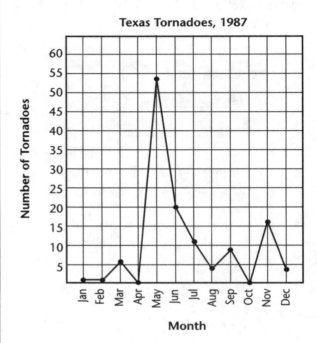

1. What is the average low temperature in Dallas during January?

   A   50°F
   B   40°F
   C   35°F
   D   30°F

2. What is the **range** of average high temperatures in the 5 Texas cities?

   A   25°F
   B   35°F
   C   40°F
   D   65°F

3. During which month were there 11 tornadoes?

   A   March
   B   June
   C   July
   D   September

4. How many more tornadoes were there in June than in October?

   A   4
   B   8
   C   10
   D   20

Probability and Statistics

Expectation: Describe characteristics of data presented in tables and graphs, including the shape and spread of the data and the middle number

The graph shows the record high temperatures for some cities in Texas. Use the graph to answer questions 1 and 2.

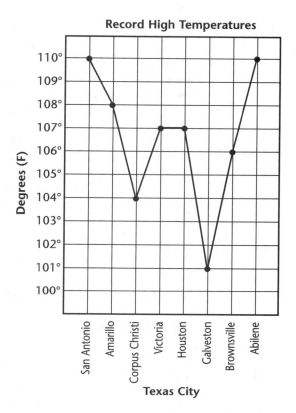

Record High Temperatures

The graph shows the number of students who participate in different sports at North Elementary School. Use the graph to answer questions 3 and 4.

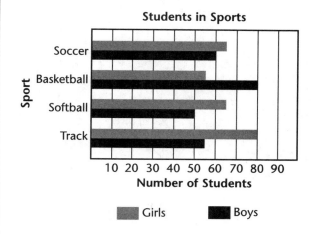

Students in Sports

3. How many girls participate in softball?

   A   50

   B   60

   C   65

   D   80

1. Which city has a record high of 104°F?

   A   San Antonio

   B   Corpus Christi

   C   Houston

   D   Galveston

4. What is the **range** in the number of girls and number of boys who participate in track?

   A   25

   B   35

   C   55

   D   80

2. What is the **range** of record high temperatures for these Texas cities?

   A   110°F

   B   30°F

   C   19°F

   D   9°F

Probability and Statistics

Expectation: Describe characteristics of data presented in tables and graphs, including the shape and spread of the data and the middle number

Mindy created a diagram to show how many students in her class had their own radios, TVs, and computers. Use the diagram to answer questions 1 and 2.

What Students Own

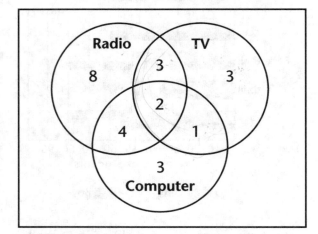

A store owner kept track of how many customers bought each of 3 new products: Pop's Pizza, Judy's Juice, and Apple Crispies. Use the diagram to answer questions 3 and 4.

New Product Sales

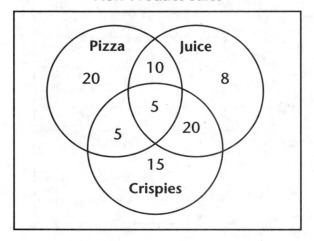

1. How many students have both a radio and a computer but no TV?

    A   2

    B   4

    C   6

    D   15

2. How many students have a TV of their own?

    A   3

    B   6

    C   7

    D   9

3. How many customers bought all 3 new products?

    Record your answer and fill in the bubbles on your answer document. Be sure to use the correct place value.

4. How many customers bought both Judy's Juice and Apple Crispies but no Pop's Pizza?

    A   20

    B   23

    C   25

    D   43

Objective 5
Exercise 16

Probability and Statistics

Expectation: Graph a given set of data using an appropriate graphical representation, such as a picture or a line

1. The chart shows the pets owned by students in Audry's class.

Kind of Pet	Number of Students
Cat	5
Dog	8
Fish	2
Cat and Dog	6
Cat and Fish	2
Dog and Fish	1
Cat, Dog, and Fish	2

Which diagram shows the same information as the chart?

A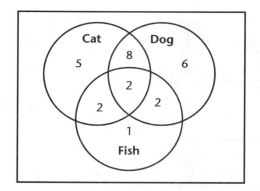

B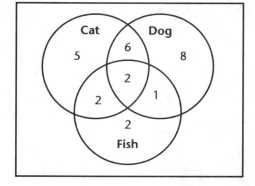

C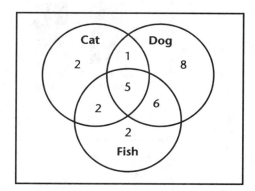

D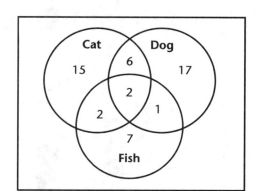

2. In PE last Friday, 25 students played volleyball, 20 students played basketball, 10 students played hockey, 15 students played tennis, and 10 students jumped rope. Which graph correctly shows the number of students who participated in each activity?

A

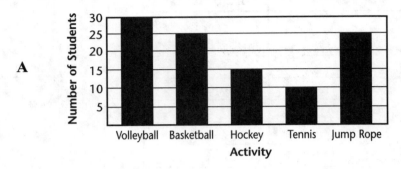

B

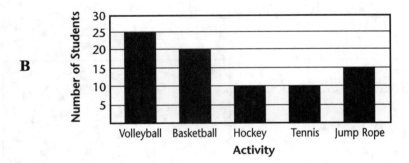

C

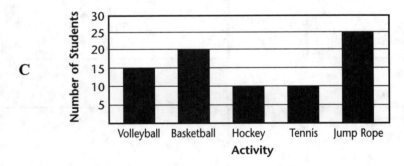

D

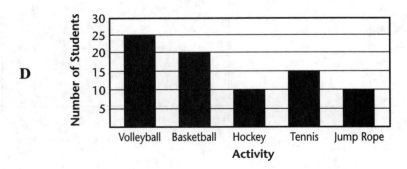

Probability and Statistics

Expectation: Graph a given set of data using an appropriate graphical representation, such as a picture or a line

3. Karen wants to buy a new bicycle. A sales clerk told Karen that she would pay from $150 to $250 for a good bicycle. Karen wants a good one, but she cannot spend more than $200. Which number line shows how much Karen could spend for a good bicycle?

A

B

C
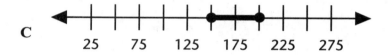

D

Probability and Statistics

Expectation: Graph a given set of data using an appropriate graphical representation, such as a picture or a line

1. Ashley counted how many students in her class were wearing clothes with 1 or more of the school colors: red, blue, and green. The chart shows the results of her count.

Color of Clothes	Number of Students
Red	10
Blue	3
Green	1
Red and Blue	5
Blue and Green	1
Red and Green	4
Red, Blue, and Green	5

Which diagram shows the same information as the chart?

A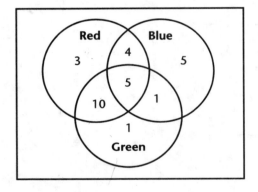

C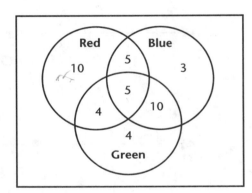

B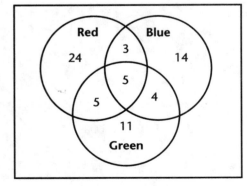

D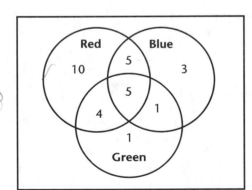

Probability and Statistics

Expectation: Graph a given set of data using an appropriate graphical representation, such as a picture or a line

2. The Tate family's wading pool is 24 inches deep. The water level is 16 inches deep now. Mr. Tate wants to add water to the pool. Which number line shows all the possible numbers of inches the water level could be if it is greater than or equal to 16 inches, but less than or equal to 24 inches?

A
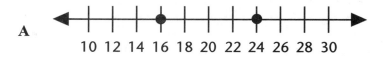

B

C

D

Probability and Statistics

Expectation: Graph a given set of data using an appropriate graphical representation, such as a picture or a line

3. Classes at Beacon Elementary held a contest to raise money for the school. The table shows how much money each class earned.

Class	K	1	2	3	4	5
Money Earned	$250	$175	$200	$300	$375	$250

If each $ sign stands for 25 dollars, which graph correctly shows the amount of money each class earned?

A

K	$$$$$$$$
1	$$$$$$
2	$$$$$$$
3	$$$$$$$$$$$
4	$$$$$$$$$$$$$$
5	$$$$$$$$

C

K	$$$$$$$$$$$$$
1	$$$$$$$
2	$$$$$$$$$
3	$$$$$$$$$$$
4	$$$$$$$$$
5	$$$$$$$$$$$$$$$

B

K	$$$$$
1	$$$
2	$$$$
3	$$$$$
4	$$$$$$
5	$$$$$

D

K	$$$$$$
1	$$$$$$$
2	$$$$$$$$$
3	$$$$$$$$$$
4	$$$$$$$$$$$
5	$$$$$$$$$$$$$$$

Objective 6

Underlying Processes and Mathematical Tools

A. Identify the mathematics in everyday situations

B. Use a problem-solving model that incorporates understanding the problem, making a plan, carrying out the plan, and evaluating the solution for reasonableness

C. Select or develop an appropriate problem-solving strategy, including drawing a picture, looking for a pattern, systematic guessing and checking, acting it out, making a table, working a simpler problem, or working backward to solve a problem

D. Relate informal language to mathematical language and symbols

E. Make generalizations from patterns or sets of examples and nonexamples

1. Jake keeps some of the statistics for the school's volleyball team as shown below.

Play	Smith	Gonzalez	Johnson	Huber
Good Pass	卌	卌 I	III	III
Bad Pass	II	III	II	IIII
Block			II	卌
Hit	III	II	I	III

Which chart correctly shows this information?

A

Play	Total
Good Pass	15
Bad Pass	11
Block	7
Hit	5

B

Play	Total
Good Pass	17
Bad Pass	11
Block	8
Hit	11

C

Play	Total
Good Pass	11
Bad Pass	11
Block	8
Hit	16

D

Play	Total
Good Pass	17
Bad Pass	11
Block	7
Hit	9

2. Mrs. Witt is a hair stylist. The calendar below shows her appointments for this week.

Monday	Ms. Dunbar 11:00–1:00
Tuesday	Mrs. Fielder 12:30–2:00
Wednesday	no appointments
Thursday	Ms. Cummings 1:00–2:00 Miss Trudy 2:00–3:30
Friday	no appointments
Saturday	no appointments

Which table below most accurately shows Mrs. Witt's work schedule for this week?

A

Day	Time Scheduled
Monday	2 hr
Tuesday	1 hr 30 min
Wednesday	
Thursday	2 hr 30 min
Friday	
Saturday	

B

Day	Time Scheduled
Monday	1 hr
Tuesday	1 hr 30 min
Wednesday	
Thursday	2 hr 30 min
Friday	
Saturday	

C

Day	Time Scheduled
Monday	2 hr
Tuesday	2 hr 30 min
Wednesday	
Thursday	2 hr 30 min
Friday	
Saturday	

D

Day	Time Scheduled
Monday	2 hr
Tuesday	1 hr 30 min
Wednesday	1 hr 30 min
Thursday	2 hr 30 min
Friday	
Saturday	

Underlying Processes and Mathematical Tools

Expectation: Identify the mathematics in everyday situations

1. Ms. Keenan gave her class a 50-question test. Each question was worth 2 points. The chart below is Ms. Keenan's record of how many questions each student correctly answered.

Josh	38
Hannah	45
Keith	47
Dylan	41
Mariah	39
Keisha	46

Based on the points received for each correct answer, which chart accurately shows each student's total grade?

A

Josh	88
Hannah	95
Keith	97
Dylan	91
Mariah	89
Keisha	96

B

Josh	76
Hannah	90
Keith	94
Dylan	82
Mariah	78
Keisha	92

C

Josh	40
Hannah	47
Keith	49
Dylan	43
Mariah	41
Keisha	48

D

Josh	58
Hannah	65
Keith	67
Dylan	61
Mariah	59
Keisha	76

2. Mr. Bevin collects stamps. He sorts them according to their dollar value as shown in the chart below.

Dollar Value	Number of Stamps
$10+	30
$5–$10	24
$1–$5	31

Mr. Bevin sells 12 of his $5–$10 stamps so he can purchase 2 more $10+ stamps. Which statement is **NOT** true after Mr. Bevin sells some of his stamps to buy others?

A He owns fewer $1–$5 stamps than $10+ stamps.

B He owns an equal number of $1–$5 stamps and $10+ stamps.

C He owns 12 $5–$10 stamps.

D He owns 20 more $10+ stamps than $5–$10 stamps.

3. Kai let several of his friends borrow money for the school book fair. He kept a record of how much money each friend borrowed.

Leo	$4.30
Sasha	~~$5.20~~ 4.00
Matt	$2.25
Lauren	~~$3.50~~ 50

The day after the book fair, Sasha gave Kai $1.20 and Lauren gave him $3. Who owes Kai the most money now?

A Sasha

B Matt

C Leo

D Lauren

1. The 2-week calendar shows Matthew's after-school activities.

Sun	Mon	Tues	Wed	Thur	Fri	Sat
	1 Karate 4–5	2	3 Piano 4–6	4	5	6 Tutoring 11–2
7	8 Karate 4–5	9	10	11	12 Tutoring 11–2	13

Which table below most accurately shows Matthew's after-school activity schedule for the 2 weeks?

A

Date	Hours
December 1	1
December 3	1
December 6	2
December 8	1
December 12	2

B

Date	Hours
December 1	1
December 3	2
December 6	3
December 8	1
December 12	3

C

Date	Hours
December 1	1
December 3	2
December 6	2
December 8	1
December 12	2

D

Date	Hours
December 1	1
December 3	2
December 6	4
December 8	1
December 12	2

2. Andrea spent an afternoon in her grandfather's convenience store. The cash register broke, so she kept a record of every sale and purchase. There was $481.87 in the cash register when it broke. Then, Mrs. Milton bought a snack for $4.60. Mr. Gregory bought gas for $14.50. And, Mr. Johnson sold the store $125.00 worth of soda cans and $100 worth of chips, which Andrea's grandfather bought with cash from the register. Which table most accurately shows the sales and purchases that Andrea recorded after the cash register broke?

A
$481.87
− $4.60
− $14.50
− $125.00
− $100.00
——————
$237.77

B
$481.87
+ $4.60
+ $14.50
+ $125.00
+ $100.00
——————
$725.97

C
$481.87
− $4.60
− $14.50
+ $125.00
+ $100.00
——————
$687.77

D
$481.87
+ $4.60
+ $14.50
− $125.00
− $100.00
——————
$275.97

1. Marcus wants to find the total amount of pretend money he has while playing a board game. Look at the problem-solving steps shown below. Arrange the steps in the best order for Marcus to find the total value of his pretend money.

   Step A: Add the total values of each type of bill.

   Step B: Count and record the number of each type of bill.

   Step C: Separate bills into groups of the same type of bill.

   Step D: Multiply the number of each type of bill by that type of bill's value.

   Which list shows the steps in the correct order?

   A B, D, A, C

   B C, B, D, A

   C C, B, A, D

   D A, B, C, D

2. Identify the equation below that models $3^4 = 81$.

   A $3 \times 3 \times 3 \times 3 = 81$

   B $9 \times 9 = 81$

   C $4 \times 4 \times 4 = 81$

   D $3(4) = 81$

3. Karlie wants to buy 1 slice of pizza, 1 lemonade, and 1 apple for lunch. She has $1.95 to spend. Karlie knows that 1 slice of pizza is $1.25. What other information is necessary for Karlie to determine how much money her lunch will cost in all?

   A The total amount of coins she has

   B The cost of 1 lemonade

   C The cost of 1 lemonade and 1 apple

   D The difference between the cost of 1 lemonade and 1 slice of pizza

4. On average, Dennis scores 12 points, not counting free throws, per basketball game. He wants to find the average number of minutes he plays for every basket he makes. What other information does Dennis need to know to find the average number of minutes played for every basket?

   A The average number of total minutes he plays in each game

   B The average number of time outs the coach takes in a game

   C The number of total minutes in a game

   D The average number of points the other players on his team make in a game

Underlying Processes and Mathematical Tools

Expectation: Use a problem-solving model that incorporates understanding the problem, making a plan, carrying out the plan, and evaluating the solution for reasonableness

Mr. Brooks keeps a record of how many items he sells from his store and at what price they were purchased. He knows that last Saturday he only sold $14 worth of socks and 3 hats for between $15 and $25 each. Use this information to answer questions 1 and 2.

1. Based on this information, which of the following statements is **NOT** true?

   A Mr. Brooks sold less than $75 worth of hats last Saturday.

   B Mr. Brooks made more money selling hats than selling socks last Saturday.

   C Mr. Brooks sold less than $100 worth of items last Saturday.

   D Mr. Brooks sold more than $100 worth of items last Saturday.

2. If we know that each hat cost the same amount of money, what additional information do we need in order to determine the exact value of each hat Mr. Brooks sold last Saturday?

   A The number of people who bought merchandise last Saturday

   B The total value of all of the merchandise Mr. Brooks sold last Saturday

   C The total value of the socks Mr. Brooks sold last Saturday

   D The number of items Mr. Brooks sold in all

3. Melanie wants to find the amount of change she should receive from a funnel-cake vendor at the fair. Look at the problem-solving steps shown below. Arrange the steps in the correct order for Melanie to find the amount of change she should receive.

   Step J: Multiply the cost of a funnel cake by the number of funnel cakes being purchased.

   Step K: Determine the cost of 1 funnel cake.

   Step L: Subtract the total cost of all the funnel cakes being purchased from the amount of money being given to the vendor.

   Step M: Determine the number of funnel cakes being purchased.

   Which list shows the steps in the correct order?

   A K, M, J, L

   B K, M, L, J

   C M, K, L, J

   D J, K, M, L

4. Alex's age and his younger brother's age together equal 30 years. Alex's age is 4 times greater than his brother's. How old are the brothers?

   A 4 and 16

   B 9 and 21

   C 3 and 12

   D 6 and 24

Underlying Processes and Mathematical Tools

Expectation: Use a problem-solving model that incorporates understanding the problem, making a plan, carrying out the plan, and evaluating the solution for reasonableness

1. Deborah wants to find the amount of time she spends in each class during the day. Her school day begins at 8:05 a.m. and ends at 3:45 p.m. She attends 6 different classes for the same amount of time each, she spends some time moving from one class to another, and she has a 35-minute lunch. What information does Deborah need in order to find the length of each class?

   A   How many days are in the school year

   B   How many students are in each class

   C   How much time she spends moving from one class to another during the day

   D   The exact time of her lunch period

2. For breakfast, Sandra is making a pitcher of orange juice from 1 can of orange-juice concentrate. The directions tell her to pour 1 can containing 12 ounces of concentrate into the pitcher. Then, she must refill the can with water and pour it into the pitcher 3 times. What additional information does Sandra need in order to find the number of people she can serve orange juice after making 1 pitcher?

   A   The total ounces of water she pours into the pitcher

   B   The amount of orange juice she needs to pour into each person's glass

   C   The total number of glasses she has

   D   The total number of people who want orange juice

3. Mr. Patel replaced the border on his bulletin board with decorative edging. He purchased 24 feet of edging, but he did not use all of it. What additional information is necessary to determine how much edging Mr. Patel used to replace the border?

   A   The area of the bulletin board

   B   The perimeter of the bulletin board

   C   The shape of the bulletin board

   D   The height of the bulletin board

4. In her garden, Rene counts the number of tomatoes on her tomato plants. She also counts the number of bell peppers on her bell-pepper plants. If Rene knows she has a total of 75 tomatoes on the tomato plants and 13 bell-pepper plants, what else does she need to know to find the average number of tomatoes on each tomato plant?

   A   The total number of bell peppers

   B   The average number of bell peppers on each bell-pepper plant

   C   The total number of tomatoes and bell peppers

   D   The total number of tomato plants

1. Theresa played in the backyard with her dog every day this week to give him exercise. The veterinarian asked Theresa to tell him the average time her dog exercised each day this week. Determine which of the following would **NOT** help Theresa answer the veterinarian's question?

   A Make a chart that lists the days of the week, and record the number of minutes spent playing each day

   B Add the daily times, and divide by the number of days they played

   C Find the area of the backyard

   D Record the starting time and stopping time each day when she plays with her dog

2. Jaime can choose to buy only 1 of 2 sets of kitchen pots. The first set contains 12 pieces and sells for $135.99. The second set contains 14 pieces and sells for $147.25. Jaime wants to buy the set that has the lowest price per individual piece. How can Jaime determine which set has the lowest price per piece?

   A Compare the answers when he divides 135.99 by 12 and divides $147.25 by 14

   B Subtract $135.99 from $147.25

   C Compare the answers when he divides 135.99 by 14 and divides $147.25 by 12

   D Subtract $135.99 from $147.25 and divide the difference by 14

3. Beau can drive his truck from the store to his house in 5 minutes. He drives at a constant speed, and he does not have to stop during the drive. Beau always drives the speed limit, which is 30 miles per hour (60 minutes). Based on this information, how can Beau find the number of miles between his house and the grocery store?

   A $5 \times (30 \div 60)$

   B 5×30

   C $30 \div 5$

   D $5 \times 30 \times 60$

4. Danny divided his bedroom into sections. The total area of the bedroom is 125 square feet. Danny allots 25% to be his sleeping space, 30% to be his study space, and the remaining area of his room to keep his guitar, bookshelves, and stereo. Determine which of the following questions could **NOT** be answered with the information provided.

   A What is the percentage of the area of the room where Danny keeps his guitar, bookshelves, and stereo?

   B What is the area of Danny's sleeping space?

   C What is the perimeter of Danny's bedroom?

   D Which designated space is the largest?

1. Mara knows the distance of each line along the outside edge of a tennis court. She also knows the height of the tennis net. Which formula can Mara use to determine the total distance around the outer edge of the tennis court?

   A   Area of a rectangle

   B   Width of a rectangle

   C   Perimeter of a rectangle

   D   Volume of a rectangle

2. Cynthia's clock says it is 12:15 p.m. When the second hand ticks from 7 seconds to 8 seconds, it moves exactly between the hour hand and minute hand. What should Cynthia do to determine the angle that the second hand and minute hand form?

   A   Divide 90 by 2

   B   Divide 15 by 2

   C   Subtract 7.5 from 15

   D   Divide 180 by 2

3. Phoebe had a bag of 24 pieces of candy. Phoebe ate 6 pieces and her brother ate 8 pieces. How can Phoebe find the fraction of candy she and her brother ate?

   A $8 + 6 = 14$

   B $\dfrac{6}{24} + \dfrac{8}{24} = \dfrac{14}{48}$

   C $\dfrac{24}{24} - \dfrac{14}{24} = \dfrac{10}{24}$

   D $\dfrac{6}{24} + \dfrac{8}{24} = \dfrac{14}{24}$

4. Marina buys 9 liters of soda from the grocery store for a party. She also buys 1 cup for each guest. Each cup can hold 400 milliliters of liquid. What should Marina do to find the number of cups she can fill with the amount of soda she bought?

   A   Multiply 1,000 by 9, and then multiply the product by 400

   B   Divide 400 by 9

   C   Divide 1,000 by 400

   D   Multiply 1,000 by 9, and then divide the product by 400

1. Eddie is in charge of cutting pieces of steel for a construction project. Each piece of steel he cuts must be 11 feet long. He must cut the steel pieces from 2 larger beams. One beam is 49 feet long and the other is 34 feet long. Determine which of the following questions could **NOT** be answered with the information provided.

   A How many 11-foot pieces of steel can Eddie cut from the 2 larger beams?

   B What is the total number of feet left from the 2 larger steel beams after Eddie cuts his 11-foot pieces?

   C What is the total length of all the 11-foot steel pieces Eddie cuts from the 2 beams?

   D How long does it take Eddie to cut the steel pieces from the 2 beams?

2. Lupita wants to make curtains to match her new bedspread. The width of her window is $3\frac{1}{4}$ feet. The width of the actual curtain must be twice the width of the window, so it can hang with pleats on the curtain rod. Determine which of the following questions could **NOT** be answered with the information provided.

   A How wide will Lupita's curtains be?

   B How long will Lupita's curtain rod be?

   C What is the area of the fabric required to make the curtains?

   D If Lupita cuts her curtains lengthwise into 2 equal pieces that each cover $\frac{1}{2}$ of the window, what will the width of each piece be?

3. A rectangular prism made of 1-inch cubes is shown below.

   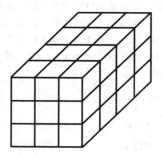

   What is the volume of this prism?

   A $3 \text{ in} \times 4 \text{ in} = 12 \text{ in}^3$

   B $3 \text{ in} \times 3 \text{ in} \times 3 \text{ in} = 27 \text{ in}^3$

   C $3 \text{ in} \times 3 \text{ in} \times 4 \text{ in} = 36 \text{ in}^3$

   D $4 \text{ in} \times 4 \text{ in} \times 4 \text{ in} = 64 \text{ in}^3$

4. Milo is delivering rolls of wrapping paper to people who bought them for his fundraiser. He has 28 rolls of wrapping paper to deliver. He knows that everyone ordered the same number of rolls, but he cannot remember how many. What other information could he use to find the number of rolls to deliver to each person?

   A The number of square feet in a roll of wrapping paper

   B The individual cost of a roll of wrapping paper

   C The total number of people who bought rolls of wrapping paper

   D The total amount of money he raised for the fundraiser

1. Theodore stayed up late each night during the weekend. On Friday night, he did not go to sleep until 2:30 a.m. On Saturday night, he did not go to sleep until 2:15 a.m. He woke up at 8:00 a.m. on both Saturday and Sunday morning. Theodore estimates that he slept 6 hours each night, for a total of 12 hours during the weekend. Compare Theodore's estimate to the actual amount of time he slept. Explain why his estimate is more or less than the actual amount of time.

    A   More, because he rounded 2:15 up

    B   Less, because he rounded 2:30 and 2:15 up

    C   More, because he rounded both times down

    D   Less, because he rounded both times down

2. Paula is 10 years old. She discovers that her age is the product of her little brothers' ages, 2 and 5. What else can she tell about these numbers?

    A   Her age equals 5 squared

    B   2 and 5 are the prime factors of her age

    C   2 is the least common factor of 5 and 10

    D $\frac{2}{10}$ equals $\frac{2}{5}$

3. Grace and her brother stand on opposite sides of the street and race to the crosswalk ahead. Because the street has the same width from beginning to end, their paths never cross. You can describe their paths as—

    A   perpendicular

    B   congruent

    C   translations

    D   parallel

4. Shani knew that she could earn money for collecting and recycling soda cans. She collected cans from home and from school. The cans she collected from home weighed 6.65 pounds. The cans she collected from school weighed 35.9 pounds. To find the total weight, Shani estimated that the cans weighed 10 and 40 pounds. Compare Shani's estimate to the actual combined weight of the cans. Explain why her estimate is more or less than their actual weight.

    A   Less, because she rounded both numbers down

    B   More, because she rounded 35.9 and 6.65 up

    C   More, because she rounded 6.65 down

    D   Less, because she rounded 35.9 up

1. Mrs. Zingaro must estimate the value of her jewelry for the insurance company. She knows her jewel necklace is worth $565 and her wedding ring is worth $895. She also knows that both pairs of jeweled earrings are worth $265 each. Mrs. Zingaro added $600 and $900, plus $300 for each pair of earrings. Compare Mrs. Zingaro's estimate to the actual value of her jewelry. Explain why Mrs. Zingaro's estimate is more or less than the jewelry's actual value.

    A   More, because she rounded all the values up

    B   Less, because she rounded 265 and 565 down and 895 up

    C   Less, because she rounded all the values down

    D   More, because she rounded 895 down

2. Charlie participated in a charity fundraiser. For every minute he jumped rope, he earned 10¢ from 43 different people. He also earned $10 from 1 donor for simply participating in the fundraiser. If Charlie jumped rope for 45 minutes, which is the most appropriate order of operations for him to use to find the total amount of money he raised?

    A   ×, ×, +

    B   ×, +, +

    C   +, +, +

    D   ÷, ÷, +

3. Ms. Guerro wants to recover the top side of the seat cushions on her dining-room chairs. To calculate how much fabric she needs, she measures the length of 1 side of a cushion. Then, she multiplies the length by the length. Finally, she multiplies the product by the number of chairs she plans to recover. Based on Ms. Guerro's calculations, what do we know about the seat cushions?

    A   They are square, and she has calculated the perimeter.

    B   They are square, and she has calculated the area.

    C   They are round, and she has calculated the area.

    D   They are trapezoids, and she has calculated the area.

4. Miss Hookstra is a school nurse. She has a large rectangular box to hold smaller square boxes of facial tissue. To find the number of square tissue boxes she can fit in the large rectangular box, she measures the number of tissue boxes that fit the depth, width, and height of the box. Miss Hookstra is measuring—

    A   area

    B   perimeter

    C   circumference

    D   volume

Objective 6
Exercise 12

1. Alicia has a collection of 30 ceramic figurines. She wants to find the individual value of each ceramic figurine. When she bought her whole collection, it was worth $375. Now, the value of the whole collection has increased by $45. If each figurine has equal value, what order of operations would she use to find the new value for each ceramic figurine?

    A ×, ×
    B ×, +
    C +, ÷
    D ÷, +

2. Henry is taking a trip with his family by car. His mother tells him that the drive will be 3 times as long as the drive to his grandparents' house. His grandparents live exactly 89.45 miles away, but he finds the value of 3 times 90 to estimate the length of the trip. Explain why Henry's estimate is more or less than the actual length of the trip.

    A Less, because he rounded the decimal down
    B More, because he rounded the decimal up
    C Less, because he multiplied by 3
    D More, because he multiplied by 3

3. The Chao family has 3 children. None of the children are more than 6 years apart in age. The age of the oldest child and the age of the youngest child equal 26 together. If the age of the third child is exactly between the oldest and youngest, how old are the children?

    A 6, 13, 20
    B 10, 13, 16
    C 10, 12, 16
    D 13, 14, 15

4. Uri works for his grandmother's shop during the summer. He earns $6 an hour for stocking the shelves. He also earns a $5 bonus each time he unloads a delivery truck. In June, Uri worked 40 hours and unloaded 4 trucks. What order of operations would he use to find the amount of money he had at the end of June?

    A ÷, ÷, +
    B ÷, ×, +
    C ×, ×, −
    D ×, ×, +

1. These are examples of shizims.

These are not examples of shizims.

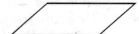

Which figure below is a shizims?

A ... B ... C ... D

2. These are examples of joppex.

These are not examples of joppex.

Which figure below is a joppex?

A B C D

3. These are examples of gizzil.

These are not examples of gizzil.

Which figure below is **NOT** a gizzil?

A B  C 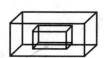 D

Underlying Processes and Mathematical Tools

*Expectation: Make generalizations from patterns or
sets of examples and nonexamples*

1. Mr. Ngyuen spent most of the morning deciding how to plant different flowers in his garden. He has decided to plant them as shown below. He leaves a space in the middle to plant a bush later.

   If Mr. Nguyen decides to continue with the flower pattern instead of planting a bush, which of the following should he plant?

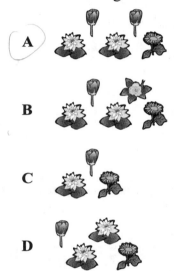

2. Portia wants to make a necklace for her best friend. She begins using random beads, as shown below.

   If Portia decides to continue with her pattern, which set of beads should she add to the necklace next?

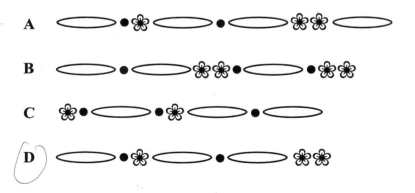

1. Lyle spent the summer with his grandparents. He kept a journal throughout the summer. Below is a list of the entry dates in his journal.

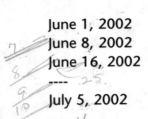

June 1, 2002
June 8, 2002
June 16, 2002
---- 25.
July 5, 2002
---- 16

Based on this pattern of dates, on which 2 dates did Lyle probably write his **fourth** and **sixth** entries?

A   June 16, 2002; July 5, 2002

B   July 16, 2002; July 28, 2002

C   July 25, 2002; July 8, 2002

D   June 25, 2002; July 16, 2002

2. Emiliano knows that joining together 2 cubes forms a rectangular prism. The figures below form a pattern. One edge of each cube measures 2 centimeters.

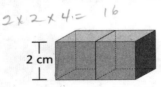
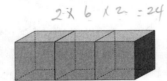
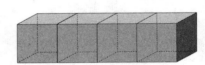

What would be the volume of the **fourth** figure in the pattern?

A   40 cm³

B   32 cm³

C   14 cm³

D   12 cm³

Answer Key

Pretest

1. B	2. D	3. C	4. A
5. A	6. B	7. B	8. B
9. D	10. D	11. A	12. C
13. B	14. C	15. B	16. A
17. B	18. B	19. B	20. A
21. C	22. C	23. D	24. D
25. B	26. C	27. B	28. C
29. B	30. B	31. C	32. D
33. C			

Objective 1

Obj. 1 Ex. 1

1. D	2. B	3. C	4. C
5. A	6. C		

Obj. 1 Ex. 2

1. B	2. D	3. C	4. D
5. C	6. B		

Obj. 1 Ex. 3

1. B	2. D	3. C	4. C
5. B	6. B		

Obj. 1 Ex. 4

1. D	2. B	3. B	4. C
5. C	6. C		

Obj. 1 Ex. 5

1. D	2. A	3. C	4. A
5. B	6. C		

Obj. 1 Ex. 6

1. C	2. C	3. C	4. A
5. A	6. B		

Obj. 1 Ex. 7

1. B	2. D	3. A	4. D
5. C	6. D		

Obj. 1 Ex. 8

1. C	2. D	3. B	4. C
5. B	6. C		

Obj. 1 Ex. 9

1. C	2. C	3. B	4. C
5. D	6. C		

Obj. 1 Ex. 10

1. B	2. C	3. A	4. B

Obj. 1 Ex. 11

1. C	2. D	3. C	4. A

Obj. 1 Ex. 12

1. A	2. C	3. D	4. C

Obj. 1 Ex. 13

1. A	2. C	3. C	4. D

Obj. 1 Ex. 14

1. C	2. B	3. C	4. D

Obj. 1 Ex. 15

1. C	2. B	3. A	4. D

Obj. 1 Ex. 16

1. C	2. D	3. C	4. A

Obj. 1 Ex. 17

1. C	2. D	3. C	4. C
5. C	6. B		

Obj. 1 Ex. 18

1. B	2. D	3. C	4. C
5. A	6. C		

Obj. 1 Ex. 19

1. D	2. A	3. 309	4. A
5. D	6. C		

Obj. 1 Ex. 20

1. A	2. B	3. C	4. A
5. D	6. A		

Obj. 1 Ex. 21

1. C	2. B	3. 216	4. D

Obj. 1 Ex. 22

1. C	2. B	3. B	4. B

Obj. 1 Ex. 23

1. A	2. B	3. D	4. C

Obj. 1 Ex. 24

1. C	2. A	3. 105	4. C

Obj. 1 Ex. 25

1. B	2. B	3. C	4. D
5. B			

Obj. 1 Ex. 26

1. B	2. C	3. A	4. B
5. C			

Obj. 1 Ex. 27

1. B	2. A	3. C	4. A
5. D			

Obj. 1 Ex. 28

1. B	2. C	3. D	4. A
5. B			

Obj. 1 Ex. 29

1. C	2. A	3. B	4. C
5. C	6. D		

Obj. 1 Ex. 30

1. A	2. D	3. D	4. B
5. C	6. D		

Obj. 1 Ex. 31

1. B	2. C	3. C	4. B
5. C	6. C		

Obj. 1 Ex. 32

1. B	2. A	3. D	4. A

Obj. 1 Ex. 33

1. B	2. D	3. D	4. C

Obj. 1 Ex. 34

1. B	2. C	3. B	4. A

Obj. 1 Ex. 35

1. D	2. B	3. B	4. C

Answer Key

Obj. 1 Ex. 36
1. C   2. A   3. B   4. B

Obj. 1 Ex. 37
1. B   2. D   3. B   4. C

Obj. 1 Ex. 38
1. C   2. C   3. D   4. C

Obj. 1 Ex. 39
1. B   2. A   3. B   4. B

Obj. 1 Ex. 40
1. C   2. D   3. B   4. C
5. C   6. B

Obj. 1 Ex. 41
1. D   2. B   3. D   4. C
5. C   6. A

Obj. 1 Ex. 42
1. C   2. B   3. C   4. D
5. A   6. B

Objective 2

Obj. 2 Ex. 1
1. B   2. D   3. C   4. C
5. D

Obj. 2 Ex. 2
1. A   2. B   3. 120   4. B
5. D

Obj. 2 Ex. 3
1. C   2. A   3. D   4. C
5. C

Obj. 2 Ex. 4
1. B   2. D   3. D   4. D
5. C

Obj. 2 Ex. 5
1. B   2. D   3. 64   4. C

Obj. 2 Ex. 6
1. D   2. B   3. C   4. D

Obj. 2 Ex. 7
1. D   2. C   3. C   4. B

Obj. 2 Ex. 8
1. D   2. B   3. D   4. C

Obj. 2 Ex. 9
1. C   2. D   3. D   4. A
5. A

Obj. 2 Ex. 10
1. C   2. A   3. D   4. B
5. C

Obj. 2 Ex. 11
1. B   2. A   3. D   4. B
5. C

Obj. 2 Ex. 12
1. D   2. C   3. B   4. A
5. D

Obj. 2 Ex. 13
1. B   2. C   3. A   4. C

Obj. 2 Ex. 14
1. B   2. D   3. A   4. D

Obj. 2 Ex. 15
1. D   2. C   3. B   4. A

Obj. 2 Ex. 16
1. B   2. C   3. D   4. A

Objective 3

Obj. 3 Ex. 1
1. C   2. A   3. C   4. B

Obj. 3 Ex. 2
1. C   2. C   3. A   4. C

Obj. 3 Ex. 3
1. D   2. D   3. B   4. C

Obj. 3 Ex. 4
1. A   2. C   3. C   4. D

Obj. 3 Ex. 5
1. B   2. C   3. D   4. D
5. A

Obj. 3 Ex. 6
1. C   2. D   3. D   4. C
5. A

Obj. 3 Ex. 7
1. D   2. B   3. C   4. D
5. B

Obj. 3 Ex. 8
1. A   2. D   3. C   4. D
5. C

Obj. 3 Ex. 9
1. B   2. D

Obj. 3 Ex. 10
1. C   2. A

Obj. 3 Ex. 11
1. B   2. D

Obj. 3 Ex. 12
1. A   2. C

Obj. 3 Ex. 13
1. C   2. D   3. B   4. C

Obj. 3 Ex. 14
1. B   2. A   3. C   4. B

Obj. 3 Ex. 15
1. C   2. D   3. D   4. B

Answer Key

Obj. 3 Ex. 16
| 1. D | 2. A | 3. C | 4. D |

Obj. 3 Ex. 17
| 1. C | 2. D | 3. B | 4. B |

Obj. 3 Ex. 18
| 1. B | 2. B | 3. D | 4. C |

Obj. 3 Ex. 19
| 1. C | 2. D | 3. D | 4. A |

Objective 4

Obj. 4 Ex. 1
| 1. D | 2. B | 3. C | 4. C |

Obj. 4 Ex. 2
| 1. B | 2. C | 3. C | 4. C |

Obj. 4 Ex. 3
| 1. D | 2. B | 3. A | 4. B |

Obj. 4 Ex. 4
| 1. D | 2. D | 3. D | 4. C |
| 5. C | 6. D |

Obj. 4 Ex. 5
| 1. A | 2. C | 3. A | 4. C |
| 5. B |

Obj. 4 Ex. 6
| 1. A | 2. D | 3. A | 4. D |
| 5. C | 6. D |

Obj. 4 Ex. 7
| 1. C | 2. A | 3. B | 4. D |
| 5. B |

Obj. 4 Ex. 8
| 1. D | 2. C | 3. A | 4. A |
| 5. C |

Obj. 4 Ex. 9
| 1. B | 2. A | 3. D | 4. A |
| 5. C |

Obj. 4 Ex. 10
| 1. C | 2. D | 3. A | 4. D |
| 5. B | 6. C |

Obj. 4 Ex. 11
| 1. C | 2. A | 3. D | 4. C |
| 5. A | 6. D |

Obj. 4 Ex. 12
| 1. D | 2. A | 3. B | 4. B |
| 5. A | 6. B |

Obj. 4 Ex. 13
| 1. C | 2. D | 3. A | 4. B |
| 5. B | 6. D |

Objective 5

Obj. 5 Ex. 1
| 1. D | 2. B | 3. C | 4. A |

Obj. 5 Ex. 2
| 1. A | 2. D | 3. C | 4. C |

Obj. 5 Ex. 3
| 1. A | 2. C | 3. A | 4. D |

Obj. 5 Ex. 4
| 1. A | 2. D | 3. B | 4. A |

Obj. 5 Ex. 5
| 1. D | 2. A | 3. C | 4. D |

Obj. 5 Ex. 6
| 1. C | 2. D | 3. D | 4. D |

Obj. 5 Ex. 7
| 1. D | 2. C | 3. C | 4. B |

Obj. 5 Ex. 8
| 1. D | 2. A | 3. C | 4. A |

Obj. 5 Ex. 9
| 1. D | 2. C |

Obj. 5 Ex. 10
| 1. A | 2. B |

Obj. 5 Ex. 11
| 1. D | 2. C |

Obj. 5 Ex. 12
| 1. C | 2. D | 3. A | 4. B |
| 5. B | 6. D |

Obj. 5 Ex. 13
| 1. C | 2. A | 3. C | 4. D |

Obj. 5 Ex. 14
| 1. B | 2. D | 3. C | 4. A |

Obj. 5 Ex. 15
| 1. B | 2. D | 3. 5 | 4. A |

Obj. 5 Ex. 16
| 1. B | 2. D | 3. C |

Obj. 5 Ex. 17
| 1. D | 2. B | 3. A |

Objective 6

Obj. 6 Ex. 1
| 1. D | 2. A |

Obj. 6 Ex. 2
| 1. B | 2. B | 3. C |

Obj. 6 Ex. 3
| 1. B | 2. D |

Obj. 6 Ex. 4
| 1. B | 2 A | 3. C | 4. A |

Obj. 6 Ex. 5
| 1. D | 2. B | 3. A | 4. D |

Answer Key

Obj. 6 Ex. 6
1. C   2. B   3. B   4. D

Obj. 6 Ex. 7
1. C   2. A   3. A   4. C

Obj. 6 Ex. 8
1. C   2. A   3. D   4. D

Obj. 6 Ex. 9
1. D   2. C   3. C   4. C

Obj. 6 Ex. 10
1. C   2. B   3. D   4. B

Obj. 6 Ex. 11
1. A   2. A   3. B   4. D

Obj. 6 Ex. 12
1. C   2. B   3. B   4. D

Obj. 6 Ex. 13
1. B   2. D   3. C

Obj. 6 Ex. 14
1. A   2. D

Obj. 6 Ex. 15
1. D   2. A

Answer Sheet A

Name _____

Date _____ Exercise _____
1. Ⓐ Ⓑ Ⓒ Ⓓ
2. Ⓐ Ⓑ Ⓒ Ⓓ
3. Ⓐ Ⓑ Ⓒ Ⓓ
4. Ⓐ Ⓑ Ⓒ Ⓓ
5. Ⓐ Ⓑ Ⓒ Ⓓ
6. Ⓐ Ⓑ Ⓒ Ⓓ
7. Ⓐ Ⓑ Ⓒ Ⓓ
8. Ⓐ Ⓑ Ⓒ Ⓓ

Date _____ Exercise _____
1. Ⓐ Ⓑ Ⓒ Ⓓ
2. Ⓐ Ⓑ Ⓒ Ⓓ
3. Ⓐ Ⓑ Ⓒ Ⓓ
4. Ⓐ Ⓑ Ⓒ Ⓓ
5. Ⓐ Ⓑ Ⓒ Ⓓ
6. Ⓐ Ⓑ Ⓒ Ⓓ
7. Ⓐ Ⓑ Ⓒ Ⓓ
8. Ⓐ Ⓑ Ⓒ Ⓓ

Date _____ Exercise _____
1. Ⓐ Ⓑ Ⓒ Ⓓ
2. Ⓐ Ⓑ Ⓒ Ⓓ
3. Ⓐ Ⓑ Ⓒ Ⓓ
4. Ⓐ Ⓑ Ⓒ Ⓓ
5. Ⓐ Ⓑ Ⓒ Ⓓ
6. Ⓐ Ⓑ Ⓒ Ⓓ
7. Ⓐ Ⓑ Ⓒ Ⓓ
8. Ⓐ Ⓑ Ⓒ Ⓓ

Date _____ Exercise _____
1. Ⓐ Ⓑ Ⓒ Ⓓ
2. Ⓐ Ⓑ Ⓒ Ⓓ
3. Ⓐ Ⓑ Ⓒ Ⓓ
4. Ⓐ Ⓑ Ⓒ Ⓓ
5. Ⓐ Ⓑ Ⓒ Ⓓ
6. Ⓐ Ⓑ Ⓒ Ⓓ
7. Ⓐ Ⓑ Ⓒ Ⓓ
8. Ⓐ Ⓑ Ⓒ Ⓓ

Date _____ Exercise _____
1. Ⓐ Ⓑ Ⓒ Ⓓ
2. Ⓐ Ⓑ Ⓒ Ⓓ
3. Ⓐ Ⓑ Ⓒ Ⓓ
4. Ⓐ Ⓑ Ⓒ Ⓓ
5. Ⓐ Ⓑ Ⓒ Ⓓ
6. Ⓐ Ⓑ Ⓒ Ⓓ
7. Ⓐ Ⓑ Ⓒ Ⓓ
8. Ⓐ Ⓑ Ⓒ Ⓓ

Date _____ Exercise _____
1. Ⓐ Ⓑ Ⓒ Ⓓ
2. Ⓐ Ⓑ Ⓒ Ⓓ
3. Ⓐ Ⓑ Ⓒ Ⓓ
4. Ⓐ Ⓑ Ⓒ Ⓓ
5. Ⓐ Ⓑ Ⓒ Ⓓ
6. Ⓐ Ⓑ Ⓒ Ⓓ
7. Ⓐ Ⓑ Ⓒ Ⓓ
8. Ⓐ Ⓑ Ⓒ Ⓓ

Answer Sheet B

Name _____

Date _____ Exercise _____

1. (A)   2. (A)   3. [grid: columns with 0-9 digits and decimal point]   4. (A)   5. (A)   6. (A)   7. (A)   8. (A)
   (B)   (B)   (B)   (B)   (B)   (B)   (B)
   (C)   (C)   (C)   (C)   (C)   (C)   (C)
   (D)   (D)   (D)   (D)   (D)   (D)   (D)

Date _____ Exercise _____

1. (A)   2. (A)   3. [grid: columns with 0-9 digits and decimal point]   4. (A)   5. (A)   6. (A)   7. (A)   8. (A)
   (B)   (B)   (B)   (B)   (B)   (B)   (B)
   (C)   (C)   (C)   (C)   (C)   (C)   (C)
   (D)   (D)   (D)   (D)   (D)   (D)   (D)

Date _____ Exercise _____

1. (A)   2. (A)   3. [grid: columns with 0-9 digits and decimal point]   4. (A)   5. (A)   6. (A)   7. (A)   8. (A)
   (B)   (B)   (B)   (B)   (B)   (B)   (B)
   (C)   (C)   (C)   (C)   (C)   (C)   (C)
   (D)   (D)   (D)   (D)   (D)   (D)   (D)